HAYTHORNWAITE. World
Philip P.J. Uniforms &
Battles in
Colour.
MILITARY. 1815-50.

355.14
9919193

Please renew/return this item by the last date shown.

So that your telephone call is charged at local rate, please call the numbers as set out below:

8\12

From Area codes 01923 or 0208:	From the rest of Herts:
Renewals: 01923 471373	01438 737373
Enquiries: 01923 471333	01438 737333
Minicom: 01923 471599	01438 737599

L32b

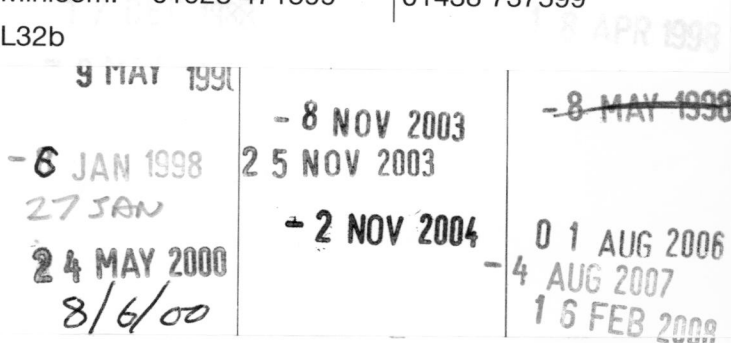

9 MAY 199(

-6 JAN 1998
27 JAN
24 MAY 2000
8/6/00

-8 NOV 2003
25 NOV 2003
-2 NOV 2004

-8 MAY 1998
0 1 AUG 2006
-4 AUG 2007
1 6 FEB 2009

HERTFO

D1491722

Please return this ... he last
date shown or ask for it to be renewed

L32/rev79

WORLD UNIFORMS
AND BATTLES
in colour
1815–50

By the same author
Uniforms of Waterloo in Colour
Uniforms of the American Civil War in Colour

WORLD UNIFORMS
AND BATTLES
in colour
1815–50

PHILIP J. HAYTHORNTHWAITE
Illustrated by
Michael Chappell

'Roll, my merry drums, march away,
Soldiers' glory lives in story,
His laurels are green when his locks are grey,
Then Hurrah for the life of a soldier.'

Popular song *c.* 1840

BLANDFORD PRESS
POOLE   DORSET

Blandford Press Ltd
Link House, West Street,
Poole, Dorset BH15 1LL

First published 1976

Copyright © 1976 Blandford Press Ltd

All rights reserved. No part of this book may
be reproduced, or transmitted in any form or
by any means, electronic or mechanical, including photocopying, recording or by any
information storage and retrieval system,
without permission in writing from the
Publisher.

HERTFORDSHIRE
COUNTY LIBRARY
355·1
9919193

Set in 10/11pt Baskerville
by Woolaston Parker Limited, Leicester
Printed in Great Britain by
Fletcher & Son Ltd, Norwich
and bound by
Richard Clay (The Chaucer Press) Ltd,
Bungay, Suffolk

ISBN 0 7137 0776 3

CONTENTS

Sequence of Black and White Plates
(Pages 179 to 183)

Plate A, Pennsylvania Militia
Plate B, Officers' Coatee, 13th Bombay Native Infantry, 1830
Plate C, French Head-dress
Plate D, British Yeomanry Head-dress
Plate E, Service Dress, Britain and U.S.A., 1846

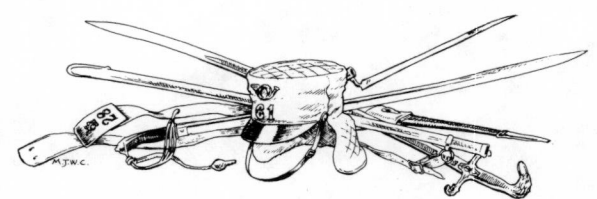

INTRODUCTION

The period of military history between the Battle of Waterloo in 1815 until the outbreak of the Crimean War in 1854 has been popularly termed 'the long peace', being the first time in centuries that the nations of Europe enjoyed a period of almost forty years without the interruption of a major war; a time when European armies were able to adopt uniforms which were freed from the underlying necessity of being functional enough for arduous campaigning.

The first sign of the rapid changes in military costume which were to occur during this period came immediately after the Battle of Waterloo, when troops of the four major Allied nations – Britain, Russia, Austria and Prussia – comprised the army of occupation of France, and mixed with members of the French Royalist forces. Developments in military costume have always depended upon the interchange between nations of uniform 'style' – items of dress copied consciously or otherwise from other nations, other armies; but for the first time ever all the major European powers were compressed into a melting-pot revolving around Parisian society, where English gentry with eighteenth-century manners mixed with Cossacks and Bashkirs from the Steppes, where kilted Highlanders walked with tight-trousered Hungarians, where the tarnished opulence of the French court mirrored the awesome foppery of the Russian Guards. Whilst the armies themselves fulfilled little useful purpose – the Russians boastfully displaying their might in a series of unending parades, the Prussians looting, the Austrians engaging in a more discreet form of smash-and-grab, the English bemusedly wandering about the city or getting drunk, the Scots babysitting or digging the gardens of their billets – the authorities responsible for the uniforms of their respective armies jealously copied, planned and adapted in an effort to outshine each other.

For the first time in years, uniforms of the ordinary troops began to be designed not for practical purposes, but for prestige reasons. Britain and Russia forsook their distinctive head-dress to copy that of Prussia, the Prussians copied the Russian legwear, while uniforms became progressively tighter and equipment less functional, until the whole process resulted in an overdressed, overdrilled and less efficient version of the mighty armies which had brought about the downfall of Napoleon.

7

While these startling innovations were in progress, while armies were becoming more ornate, the so-called 'Holy Alliance' of European monarchs which arose from the ashes of the Napoleonic Wars was cracking at the seams. A succession of political upheavals, coupled with a decline in the already often wretched living-standards of the mass of the population, and the resulting growth of republican and democratic ideals, meant that the armies of Europe had to be utilised for the most distasteful task ever given to soldiers, the duty now known as 'internal security'. Instead of fighting in the open field against a recognisable enemy as they had been trained, the Napoleonic War veterans were deployed in the suppression and prevention of insurrection, or used for political reasons as the great powers interfered in the affairs of smaller states.

These operations – which involved anything from the arrest of troublemakers and democrats to full-scale pitched battles against organised opposition – climaxed in the 'year of revolution', 1848, when it seemed that the forces of disaffection had masterminded a general revolt in the so-called 'oppressive' states. As a welcome break from these security duties, however, the armies of three nations – Britain, France, and Russia – had a chance to see some genuine soldiering, in their far-flung colonies. Service in tropical areas not only resulted in the regiments thus employed becoming efficient, fighting organisations for the first time since 1815, but also brought back the modified, more comfortable and infinitely more practical 'campaign dress' which had been largely foresaken in 'peace-time' Europe. It was from these 'colonial' uniforms, and from the Crimean War which finally marked the total collapse of the always-improbable 'Holy Alliance', that the first steps were taken in the deliberate design of uniforms suited to extended operations in the field, rather than primarily for 'show'.

The internal troubles of Europe, however, provoked another change in the theories on military dress; by 1848, certain types of uniform – and even hairstyle – had become associated with political philosophy. Republicans and democrats could be identified by their loose 'smocks', a superbly functional garment owing its inspiration to labourers' clothing. In Hungary and Germany the open-necked shirts and low-crowned, wide-brimmed felt hats with flowing plumes, copied from the 'Bohemian' style of the avant-garde society, were evidence of revolutionary ideals, and contrasted strongly with the top hats and starched collars so inseparably linked with the autocratic 'establishment'. The French – who generously allowed themselves two revolutions in this period (1830 and 1848) – provided another symbol of liberty in the cloth 'képi' head-dress and loose clothing.

The great wave of romanticism which swept through Europe also inspired military campaigns in the widespread support for the 'wars of liberation', classically in Poland and Greece, and not only gave the radicals an identifiable dress, but began also to influence their 'oppressors'. Nicholas I of Russia almost certainly designed the spiked helmet, better known by its German name of 'pickelhaube', but the prototype (according to a popular and perhaps apocryphal story) was seen by Frederick William IV of Prussia, who copied it so quickly that his army was wearing the helmet before the Russians had issued theirs! By 1848 it was the standard head-dress for both Prussian and Russian armies, and, probably due to the efforts of Prince Albert, had made its appearance in the British army. In the revolutions of 1848 the spiked helmet became a symbol of repression, a reputation which, after a barrage of propaganda during the period and later in World War I, it still shares today with the jackboot.

A classically 'romantic' and political dress was worn by Garibaldi's 'Legione Italiana', a corps of dedicated republicans proud to be identified as such by their uniforms. This marked an at times blatant use of politically-symbolic costume – which has continued to the present day (the classic case being contemporary Chinese dress) – but occasionally descended to the level of farce. The composer Liszt, for example, ran into trouble with the Karlsruhe police for wearing a 'democratic hat', while in 1846 Prussian postmen were prohibited from wearing moustaches, so that they would not be mistaken for republicans, socialists or fugitive radicals!

After the five great powers – who were copying uniforms from each other – came the myriad smaller states, the vast majority of which slavishly copied one of the large power-blocks, some actually wearing uniforms manufactured by a 'protecting' power. The German states dressed partly in Prussian and partly in Austrian styles, though Bavaria retained a more traditional uniform, and even had her copyists, notably Greece; the Italian states used a bewildering variety of Prussian, Austrian and French styles coupled with some archaic Napoleonic costume and native innovations; Scandinavia retained some traditional features but gradually absorbed Germanic styles. Ironically, Polish troops dressed in Russian style while every European army contained Lancers dressed in traditional Polish costume, and Spain produced her contribution to the development of uniform in the cloth beret, a favourite head-dress during the Carlist Wars but later forsaken for a French-style shako.

Apart from the European nations and their colonies, there remained the New World. The United States, wearing in 1815 a uniform which was British in style, followed the general European trend, going from 'Belgic' shako to bell-topped and then to 'stovepipe' patterns, but at the same time evolving a dress of her own, culminating in the 'fatigue uniform' worn in the Mexican War and on the frontier. Mexico herself, in common with many central and South American countries, chose the most ornate dress uniforms imaginable, copied originally from Napoleonic styles but embellished to a degree never even seen in the dandified days of Murat, King of Naples, the famed 'clothes-horse' of the 1st Empire. A popular story illustrates the degree of flamboyance reached by some Latin American states: when the President and Commander-in-Chief of Mexico, General Lopez de Santa Anna, was captured after the Battle of San Jacinto, a pair of his epaulettes was 'appropriated' by a quick-witted Texan – who melted them down to make a set of silver spoons! At the same time as these gorgeous uniforms were in use, however, the abysmally-poor, conscripted peasantry of Latin American armies had to be content with ragged civilian dress or tawdry, coarse and badly-produced fatigue uniforms.

To attempt a comprehensive survey of world-wide uniforms during the most decorative period ever within the bounds of one volume is clearly beyond the realms of possibility. What can be done, however, is to show a *representative* selection of uniforms worn by the major (and costume-wise most influential) armies, showing the many and varied alterations which transpired during the ill-named 'long peace', together with a selection of uniforms from the smaller states, and to illustrate either how the designers copied and modified existing, foreign patterns or how, in a few enterprising cases, devised their own. In addition to charting the never-ending interchange of uniform-styles, the functional 'working dress' evolved in the colonies and frontier areas, as well as the politically-inspired costumes worn in the European insurrections, are also shown.

Although there were no campaigns on the scale of the Napoleonic Wars during our period, the political ideologies arising from 'romantic' ideals ensured that certain campaigns received more publicity (in an age of widening news media) than had some battles of the Napoleonic Wars; the European 'crusade' to help in the Greek War of Independence, which enmeshed the archetypal romantic figure of the age, Lord Byron, and the hysterical reception in the United States of news about the War of Texan Independence provide typical examples. Other wars had far-reaching effects which influenced the foreign policy of involved nations, which in turn led to more serious conflict in the future. And, important in the development of military costume, wars which appealed to popular, national or ideological sympathy encouraged the adoption of civilian and ultimately military dress associated with the heroes of the time. In the following text, each important war is catalogued as briefly as possible, and the uniforms associated with it or arising from it are then described; in this manner, it is hoped that the generally unfamiliar military history of the period can be seen in greater clarity, and the resulting developments in uniforms can be better understood.

Some 'dress regulations' of the era described the official-pattern uniforms very precisely, but at times they are only of limited help to the uniform enthusiast; for example, the description of a shako as 'of regulation pattern, to be seen at the Adjutant-General's office' is of little value. Some regiments displayed great initiative in evolving their own individual patterns of uniform, a feature typified by the kaleidescopic variety of musicians' dress to be seen throughout Europe, while other official regulations were often so vague – or non-existent in any workable form – that there were great varieties of interpretation. Even in an army as comparatively red-tape bound as the British, only the impending visit of a staff officer or another representative of officialdom would provoke an earnest attempt to present a completely 'regulation' appearance; for example, in the mid-1830's an unfortunate tailor received the following curt missive:

'Major Gillman (69th) begs to acquaint Mr Webb that as there is now a General in this town he is afraid to wear these Epaulettes . . . Major G. will therefore thank Mr W. to take them back and send him another pair something Regulation – my Epaulettes always have 21 *large* bullions and a little longer than those I send back . . .'

The illustrations are based, many directly, upon contemporary portraits, pictures and prints of established accuracy; though a number may seem to contain unusual features or to deviate from recognised patterns, they have all been checked with the original sources. Others are based upon more modern sources, but only those of accepted accuracy and knowingly based upon original material; extant items of equipment and contemporary written descriptions have also been consulted.

1 a) Private, Light Company, 1st Foot Guards, Service Dress, 1815.
  b) Field Officer, Battalion Company, 30th Foot, 1816.

France

2 a) Grenadier, Royal Guard (ex-Imperial Guard), 1815.
  b) Officer, Gendarmes du Roi, Full Dress, 1815-16.

3 a) Fusilier Officer, 5th Infantry Regiment (4th East Prussian), Full Dress, 1815.
  b) Officer, 5th (Brandenburg) Dragoons (Regiment Prinz Wilhelm), Full Dress, 1815.

Russia

4 a) Private, Grenadier Regiment Pavlovski, Full Dress (Summer), 1815.
   b) Trooper, Don Cossacks, 1815.

5 a) Trumpeter, 10th Hussars (Stipsicz Regiment), 1815.
  b) Officer, 51st Infantry (Regiment Gabriel Spleny), 1815.

France

6 a) Fusilier, Departmental Legion, 1816.
  b) Trooper, 11th Chasseurs à Cheval (Régiment de l'Isère), 1818.

7 a) Grenadier, 7th Regiment, Garde Royale (1st Swiss), Full Dress, 1817.
  b) Musician, 8th Regiment, Garde Royale (2nd Swiss), Full Dress, 1817.

France

8 a) Trooper, Cuirassiers of the Garde Royale, 1820.
   b) Trumpeter, 3rd Dragoons (Régiment la Garonne), 1818.

9 a) Officer, 2nd Dragoons (Regiment König von Bayern), 1825.
   b) Officer, Merveldt Uhlans, 1818.

10 a) Baden – Officer, Garde du Corps, 1824.
    b) Hamburg – Private, Burgwehr, 1815.

11 a) Sergeant, Battalion Company, 2nd Foot Guards, 1821.
   b) Officer, Grenadier Company, 2nd Foot Guards, 1821.

12 a) Officer, 16th Lancers, Full Dress, 1839.
     b) Officer, 9th Lancers, Review Order, 1820.

13 a) N.C.O., 2nd Life Guards, 1833.
   b) Officer, 2nd Life Guards, 1827.

14 a) Sergeant, 13th Light Infantry, Summer Dress, 1833.
    b) Field Officer, 68th Light Infantry, 1829.

15 a) Private, Marines, Undress, 1829.
   b) Trooper, 8th Dragoons, 1827.

France

16 a) Officer, 8th Regiment, Garde Royale (2nd Swiss), 1829.
   b) Drum-Major, 7th Regiment, Garde Royale (1st Swiss), 1830.
   c) Bugler, Light Company, Infantry, 1828.

17 a) Captain, 'Flanquers', 15th Infantry, 1823.
   b) Trooper, 6th Hussars, 1823.

Papal States

PRIMO
REGGIMENTO
CARABINIERI
PONTICI

18 a) Trumpeter, Elite Company, 1st Regiment, Papal Carabiniers, 1826.
   b) Officer, Elite Company, 1st Regiment, Papal Carabiniers, 1826.

19 a) Drummer, Guard Grenadiers, Full Dress, 1831.
    b) Private, 'Flanquers' 8th Infantry, 1831.

Belgium

20 a) Officer, Tirailleurs Liègois (Luikse Tirailleurs), 1830.
   b) Officer, Civil Guard, 1831.
   c) Private, Bataillon de l'Escaut (Bataljon van de Schelde), 1837.

21 a) Voltigeur, 4th Infantry Regiment, 1826.
   b) Officer, 1st Lancers, 1830.

22 a) Sandomir Volunteers, 1830-31.
    b) Podlasie Volunteers, 1830-31.

23 a) Bandmaster, Royal Marines, 1828.
   b) Officer, Royal Marine Artillery, 1840.

24 a) Sergeant, 14th Light Dragoons, 1832.
    b) Officer, 3rd Foot Guards, 1832.

25 a) Officer, Royal Artillery, Undress, 1828.
   b) Officer, Battalion Company, 15th Foot, 1832.
   c) Sergeant, Light Company, 46th Foot, Undress, 1837.

26 a) Trumpeter, 11th Hussars, Marching Order, 1845.
    b) Officer, 10th Hussars, Full Dress, 1833.

27 a) Officer, Worcestershire Yeomanry, 1834.
    b) Officer, West Somerset Yeomanry, 1846.

Britain

28 a) Officer, 60th King's Royal Rifle Corps, 1833.
    b) Private, Rifle Brigade, 1849.

29 a) Officer, Light Company, 72nd Highlanders, 1840.
   b) Officer, Battalion Company, 78th Ross-shire Buffs, 1834.

Prussia

30 a) N.C.O., 1st Guard Landwehr Regiment, Service Dress, 1837.
b) N.C.O., 2nd Foot Guards, Full Dress, 1830.

31 a) Trumpeter, 1st Chasseurs à Cheval, 1833.
   b) Officer, Guides de la Meuse (Gids van de Maas), 1831.

Russia

32 a) Officer, Tartars of the Guard, 1835.
   b) Trooper, Guard Hussar Squadron, Service Dress, 1835.

33 a) Officer, Chevaliers Guards, Full Dress, 1835.
   b) Drum-Major, Palace Guard, 1835.

34 a) Trooper, Guard Lancer Squadron, Service Dress, 1835.
    b) N.C.O., Grenadier Regiment, Pavlovski, Service Dress, 1835.

35 a) Overjäger (N.C.O.), Fyenske Infanterie, 1837.
    b) Officer, Livgarde til Hest (Lifeguard), 1837.

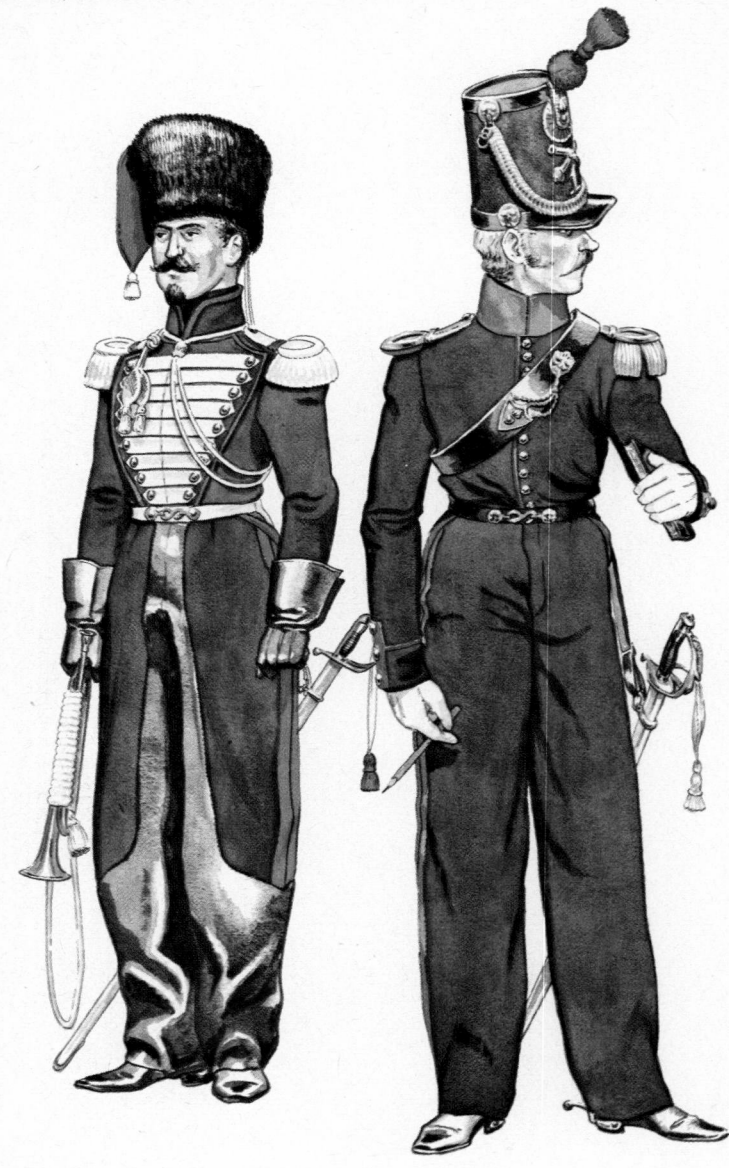

36 a) Papal States – Trumpeter, Artillery of the Foreign (Swiss) Brigade, 1834.
    b) Switzerland – Officer, Artillery, Canton Zürich, 1837.

37 a) Trooper, 2nd Lancers, 1840.
    b) Private, Artillery Train, Guard Royale, 1824.

38 a) Grenadier, Légion d'Etranger, Service Dress (Spain), 1837.
   b) Officer, Light Infantry, 1830.

39 a) Trooper, Navarrese Cavalry, 1838.
b) Officer, Arlaban Hussars, 1838.
c) Trooper, Guipzucoan Cavalry, 1838.

40 a) Officer, Mounted Chasseurs, 1820.
    b) Trooper, Horse Grenadiers, with the Banner of the Army of the Andes, 1817.

41 a) 2nd Sergeant, 5th Chasseurs, Summer Dress, 1826.
    b) Colonel, 16th Lancers, 1826.
    c) Trooper, 3rd Cuirassiers, 1826.

42 a) Argentina – Private, 1st Infantry Battalion 'Patricios', Full Dress, 1842.
b) Brazilian Empire – Trumpeter, National Guard Hussars, Full Dress (Winter), 1840.

43 a) Sergeant, Grenadier Company, Infantry, 1827.
    b) Officer, Artillery, 1827.

44 a) Trooper, Dragoons, Service Dress, 1836.
   b) Ordnance Sergeant, 1836.

45 a) Mexico – Sergeant, Batallon de Matamoros, 1836.
   b) Texas – Private, New Orleans Greys, 1836.

Republic of Texas

46 a) Officer, Ordnance Department, Service Dress (Winter), 1839.
    b) 1st Sergeant, Infantry, Marching Order, 1839.
    c) Sergeant, Marine Corps, Fatigue Dress, 1839.

47 a) Private, Regular Infantry, Service Dress (Summer), 1837.
   b) Lieutenant, Regular Infantry, Full Dress (Winter), 1826.

48 a) Sepoy, Nasseri Battalion, 1816.
    b) Trumpeter, Skinner's Horse (1st Bengal Local Horse), 1828.

49 a) Sergeant, Light Company, 28th Bengal Native Infantry, 1846.
   b) Corporal, 1st Madras (European) Fusiliers, Service Dress, 1846.
   c) Band-Sergeant, Madras Native Infantry, 1846.

Indian Army

50 a) Officer, 1st Madras Light Cavalry, 1848.
    b) Officer, 6th Bengal Irregular Cavalry, 1849.

51 a) Officer, 3rd Light Dragoons, Sikh War, 1845.
   b) Private, Light Company, 29th Foot, Sikh War, 1845-46.

52 a) Bavaria – Colonel, 1st Cuirassiers, 1835, (Prince Charles of Bavaria).
    b) Prussia – Officer, Guard Hussars, 1845.

53 a) Trooper, 3rd Dragoons, 1843.
    b) Officer, 2nd Schützen (Rifle) Battalion, Summer Dress, 1843.

54 a) Trooper, Paris Republican Guard, 1848.
    b) Grenadier, Infantry, 1845.

55 a) Trooper, 1st Calatrava Lancers, 1845.
   b) Trumpeter, 1st King's Cuirassiers, 1845.

56 a) Officer, 2nd Dragoon Guards, 1845.
   b) Trooper, 1st Life Guards, 1849.

57 a) Mexico – Private, Batallon de San Blas (Active Coast Guards), 1847.
    b) U.S.A. – Private, Infantry, Service Dress, 1847.

U.S.A.

58 a) Trooper, Dragoons, Service Dress, 1847.
   b) Private, 1st Mississippi Rifle Volunteers, 1847.

59 a) Duchy of Modena – Private, Reali Cacciatori Scelti del Frignano (Royal Rifles of Frignano), Full Dress, 1847.
b) Papal States – Private, Swiss Guard, Undress, 1828.

60 a) Sardinia – 2nd Lieutenant with Colours, 18th Infantry Regiment, (Acqui Brigade), 1847.
   b) Parma – Captain, Guard Grenadiers, Full Dress, 1849-50.

61 a) Piedmont – Officer, 16th Infantry, Campaign Dress, 1849.
     b) Milan – Officer, Milan Civic Guard, 1848.

Roman Republic

62 a) Private, Legione Italiana, 1st Uniform, 1849.
  b) Lancer, Legione Italiana, 1849.
  c) Private, Legione Italiana, 2nd Uniform, 1849.

63 a) 'Seressaner', (Border Infantry), 1848.
    b) Private, 2nd Battalion, Gradisca Border Infantry Regiment, (No. 8), 1848.

France

64 a) Carabinier Trumpeter, 22nd Light Infantry, Service Dress, 1849.
    b) Voltigeur, 22nd Light Infantry, Service Dress, 1849.

EUROPEAN UNIFORMS, 1815

Apart from minimal changes of badges and insignia in the French army following the first abdication of Napoleon in 1814, the combatant nations embarked upon the 1815 campaign in the same uniforms which they had worn during the latter years of the Napoleonic Wars, and even by the time of the Battle of Waterloo many regiments were wearing uniforms officially superseded years before. The 'time-lag' between the authorisation of a uniform and its actual adoption is one of the most difficult points to determine; an example is provided by some of the Nassau troops at Waterloo, who fought in the uniforms of their time as part of the Confederation of the Rhine, while some Prussian regiments as late as 1816 were wearing the hastily-produced uniforms issued in 1813.

As mentioned in the Introduction, it was the occupation of Paris, with troops of five nations in the closest proximity, which began the period of uniform-changes which afflicted – and graced – every army. Whereas the Prussians, Russians and Austrians invariably paraded in new, smart uniforms, most contemporary observers remarked on the meanness and untidiness of the British troops, who were still wearing the uniforms in which they had fought – and bled – in the previous months. One of the most famous observers during the early months of the Occupation was Captain Mercer of the British Royal Horse Artillery, whose writings (though influenced by the traditional English disdain of all things foreign) nevertheless reflect the embarrassment felt by many English officers when they compared their own travel-stained and shabby dress with the gorgeous creations worn by the other Allied nations. Perhaps Mercer was a little over-prejudiced against the Austrians and Russians in particular, since one of the former tried to follow him home, a Russian even ogling Mrs Mercer so that she became 'squeamish, and [was] obliged to lie down . . .' Nevertheless, his remarks are worthy of note.

All the foreign troops, Mercer wrote, 'are uncommonly well dressed in new clothes, smartly made, setting the men off to the greatest advantage – add to which their coiffure of high broad-topped shakos, or enormous caps of bear-skin. Our . . . army appeared . . . in the same clothes in which they had marched, slept and fought for months. The colour had faded to a dusky brick-dust hue; their coats, originally not

77

very smartly made, had acquired by constant wearing that loose easy set so characteristic of old clothes, comfortable to the wearer, but not calculated to add grace to his appearance . . . their cap is the meanest, ugliest thing ever invented . . . our infantry appeared to the utmost disadvantage – dirty, shabby, mean and very small'. This opinion was voiced by the other Allied nations present; when one eminent personage said as much to the Duke of Wellington, the Duke could only reply that his troops might look wretched, 'but your Majesties will find none who fight so well.'

That latter remark was probably true, but nevertheless they did compare badly in appearance to the others; of the Russian Guards, Mercer noted, 'a finer body of men can scarcely be imagined; but to me their padded breasts and waspish waists appeared preposterous . . . smart as they are on parade, are the dirtiest slovens in the world off it: the usual costume . . . is a dirty forage-cap, as dirty a grey greatcoat, generally gathered back by the waist-straps . . . dirty linen trousers, shoved up at the bottom by the projection of the unlaced half-boot . . .'; the Austrians, 'heavily-built and boorish', with their Garde du Corps 'not a little ridiculous' in their old-fashioned uniforms with cocked hats; while he found the Prussians, off parade, in 'most slovely (even beggarly) déshabille'.

European Uniforms 1815 (Plates 1-5)

1. Britain:
  a) Private, Light Company,
    1st Foot Guards,
    Service Dress, 1815.
  b) Field Officer,
    Battalion Company,
    30th Foot, 1816.

The Guardman's uniform illustrated in this plate conforms to the 1812 regulations, with the much-maligned but nevertheless quite handsome 'Belgic' shako and the short-tailed jacket. British infantry battalions were divided into eight 'battalion' and two 'flank' companies, the latter consisting of one company of grenadiers and one of light infantry; the various companies were distinguished by the colouring of the shako-plume (white for grenadiers, white over red for 'battalion' companies and green for light infantry), by the 'wings' of the flank companies, and by the shako-cords, some light companies having green instead of the usual white. After 1814 many light companies were further distinguished by the addition of a small bugle-horn badge to the shako. Regimental identification – other than badges and insignia – was indicated by the facing colour borne on the collar, cuffs, shoulder-straps and (in the Foot Guards) flank company 'wings', and by the colouring, spacing and shape of the lace loops on the cuffs, breast and pockets of the jacket. Officers wore metallic lace and epaulettes (wings for flank company officers) and the universal crimson sash. It was more usual to wear the gaiters under the overalls, but one source shows them as illustrated.

The 1st Guards were granted the title 'Grenadier' in 1815, to commemorate their defeat of the Grenadiers of the French Imperial Guard at Waterloo – even though they did not defeat the Imperial Guard column single-handed and in any case it is doubtful whether their adversaries were Grenadiers! Nevertheless, the whole regiment was granted the right to wear the bearskin cap formerly reserved for regimental Grenadier companies in full dress.

The officer of the 30th (Cambridgeshire) Regiment – his 'field' rank indicated by two epaulettes – is shown in a uniform of the same pattern as that worn at Waterloo, plus the first innovation introduced to improve the appearance of the British army during the Occupation – the bell-topped 'Regency' shako, styled on Prussian lines. The plume, in the same colours as before, was lengthened to create an impression of height, and officers' caps were heavily laced in the regimental colour. Shako-plates were of varied pattern, though crowned discs were the most usual, the plate being set on a rosette of lace, and chinscales were another innovation. Other regimental variations not common to all caps were turned-up back-peaks and

briefly-worn cap-lines. Caps of the other ranks had shorter plumes, no lace, and brass plates bearing the regimental number, sometimes with the addition of a grenade or bugle-horn badge for flank companies. Officers of light companies and light infantry – whose 'stovepipe' caps were replaced by the new pattern – had large bugle-horn badges on the front. Authorised in August 1815, the new shako was not general issue until the following year.

Even before the introduction of the 'Regency' shako, however, one branch of the British army attracted much attention. Parisian ladies, much intrigued by the kilts of the Highlanders, persisted in enquiring what (if anything) was worn underneath. On occasion the Highlanders showed them! Even the Czar was fascinated by the Highland regiments, and three Highlanders were presented to him for a close inspection. Sergeant Campbell of the 79th recorded that the Czar 'examined my hose, gaiters, legs and pinched my skin, thinking I wore something under my kilt, and had the curiosity to lift my kilt to my navel, so that he might not be deceived'!

2. France:

a) Grenadier, Royal Guard (ex-Imperial Guard), 1815.

b) Officer, Gendarmes du Roi, Full Dress, 1815–16.

The Gendarmes du Roi, a unit of the 'Maison du Roi' recreated by Louis XVIII after an interval of almost thirty years, wore a uniform of extreme opulence, equalled only by those of the companies of 'Mousquetiers', whose archaic dress included cuirass-shaped cloth tabards emblazoned with the flaming cross device reminiscent of the days of Richelieu. The Maison du Roi, a largely aristocratic body recruited by nepotism and sycophancy, was intensely disliked by the 'real' French army which had fought under Napoleon. When the need arose for an élite, Royal bodyguard upon Napoleon's return from Elba, the gorgeously-dressed Maison du Roi fell somewhat short of requirements, as had been expected by all those experienced enough to realise the difference between overdressed parade-ground soldiers and hardened veterans.

The Royal Guardsman illustrated wears the uniform of Napoleon's Imperial Guard, with only the cockade on the head-dress changed from tricolor to Bourbon, and the Imperial symbols on the cartridge-box obscured by a white fabric cover with black-painted symbols, and a large grenade with four smaller ones in the corners. The ex-Imperial Guardsmen changed their cockades after the abdication of 1814, reverting to the tricolor at the beginning of the 'Hundred Days'; again briefly reformed as the Royal Guard after Waterloo, the entire body – or at least those who had survived the campaign and had not deserted afterwards – was finally disbanded in the autumn of 1815 in a series of emotional parades. Beginning with the 1st Grenadiers on 11 September, the disbandments continued: the 2nd Grenadiers on the 16th, the 3rd and 4th Grenadiers (only 440 men between them) on the 24th; the 3rd Chasseurs (only 184) on 1 October and so on

until 25 November, when the Grenadiers à Cheval made their final parade. It marked the end of the French army's greatest era.

The bicorn hat with carrot-shaped plume – normally reserved for undress uniform – was often worn on campaign, being preferred to the bearskin for its greater comfort. The classic Imperial Guard head-dress, the bearskin cap, was reserved for dress occasions and often donned immediately prior to going into action. The greatcoat was often worn over the 'habit–veste' coat, and the epaulettes worn on the coat. Service chevrons of 'aurore' wool were worn on the left upper arm, the oldest veterans of the Imperial Guard wearing three, indicating between twenty and twenty-five years' service. The figure is shown in regulation dress, but the shortages which afflicted the French army in 1815 meant that many members of the Imperial Guard were dressed, of necessity, in anything available.

The reputation of the Royal Army – so different from that which fought for Napoleon – was at a miserably low ebb during the Occupation; the over-elaborate uniforms they wore may have been a way of compensating for their poor reputation. An example of how little they were esteemed by the occupying powers is shown by the cavalier manner in which Royalist officers were treated by their counterparts in the Allied armies; on one occasion a French general made an official complaint about the way in which an English subaltern had knocked him bodily off the pavement, into the road!

3. Prussia:

a) Fusilier Officer, 5th Infantry Regt (4th East Prussian), Full Dress, 1815.

b) Officer, 5th (Brandenburg) Dragoons (Regt Prinz Wilhelm), Full Dress, 1815.

This plate shows the full dress uniform of the Prussian army, only seen after the end of the 1815 campaign. The only difference between this uniform and that worn on active service was in head-dress, which was usually covered with a black oilskin 'waterproof'. The infantry shako was basically the same for all companies of a battalion, except for the front plate, Grenadiers having a large eagle badge, Musketeers the Royal cypher (both these in brass), and Fusiliers a lace rosette. In parade dress, a black plume was worn by all except Musketeers; other ranks' shakos lacked the chains and lace of the officers' pattern. Officers wore a longer-tailed version of the 'Kollet' coat than did the rank and file, shown here with the closed collar and epaulettes introduced in 1813 but not in universal use by the time of Waterloo. Fusilier officers carried sabres, but those of Grenadiers and Musketeers normally carried straight-bladed swords. Regimental identification was indicated by the colouring of the collar, cuffs and shoulder-straps, each Prussian province being allocated a colour, viz: East Prussia, brick red; West Prussia, crimson; Pomerania, white; Brandenburg, scarlet; Silesia, lemon yellow; Magdeburg, light blue; Westphalia, rose-pink; Rheinish, crab-red. These colours were borne on the collar and cuffs, while the shoulder-straps indicated the seniority of the unit in the provincial list, viz: 1st Regiment, white; 2nd scarlet, 3rd yellow, 4th light blue. It could therefore be seen at a glance that the regiment illustrated, having brick-red facings and light blue shoulder-straps, was the 4th Regiment of East Prussia.

Dragoons wore shakos of similar pattern, those of the rank and file bearing an 'eagle' plate instead of the cockade of the officers, the tall plume (of wool for the rank and file) being reserved for parade dress. On active service, the ornaments were removed and the shako enclosed in a black 'waterproof'. Officers wore a coatee known as a 'Leibrock', while the other ranks had a not dissimilar 'Kollet'. Popular wear, however, was a thigh- or knee-length greatcoat-type garment known as a 'Litewka'. Both Kollet and Litewka were of the traditional Prussian light blue with regimental facings (normally worn only on the collar and shoulder-straps of the Litewka) as follows: 1st Regiment crimson, 2nd and 7th white, 3rd and 4th scarlet, 5th black, 6th rose-pink, 8th yellow. Buttons were brass for the 3rd, 5th and 7th and white metal for the remainder. Both officers are shown wearing the traditional silver and black lace sashes.

4. Russia:
a) Private,
Grenadier Regiment
Pavlovski,
Summer Full Dress, 1815.
b) Trooper,
Don Cossacks, 1815.

The uniform of the Pavlovski Regiment was of regulation pattern, with distinctions worn in full dress not common to ordinary line infantry uniforms, in particular the 'Guard' pattern lace on the collar and cuffs, and the coloured lapels; the ordinary Russian jacket, though double-breasted, was buttoned-over to show a plain green front, the regulations introducing single-breasted uniforms not yet having come into effect. The one-piece 'gaiter-trousers' were replaced by overalls in winter. Officers were distinguished by gold lace and epaulettes, silver sashes with interwoven orange and black lines, white breeches with black knee-boots, gorgets and straight-bladed swords, and gilt buttons (the other ranks had copper buttons). N.C.O.s had laced collars and cuffs, and sword-knots of orange and black. Equipment was of the standard Russian pattern with the cartridge-box bearing a brass Star of the Order of St Andrew, and four small grenades in the corners.

The most remarkable feature of the uniform, however, was the large, brass-fronted, mitre-shaped Grenadier cap which dated from the eighteenth century; although a remarkably archaic head-dress, it was worn by the Prussian Guards in full dress until World War I, and can even be found in the Bundeswehr today. The version worn by the Pavlovski Regiment bore the Imperial Russian arms on the front plate, with a red cloth rear, piped white, and a white panel at the back bearing brass grenade badges. N.C.O.s wore pompoms of quartered orange and black.

The cossack illustrated wears a uniform which is about the nearest thing to a 'regulation' dress which ever existed among these most feared members of the Allied armies, whose reputation for cruelty preceded them into France. All manner of uniforms – often principally civilian dress with issued, looted or captured items of head-dress and equipment – were worn, though the 'baggy' trousers and fur cap were a common feature. The cossack illustrated (taken from an eye-witness sketch) carried a regulation sabre, though 'native' swords and lances were frequently used, many cossacks accumulating weapons as a campaign progressed until they resembled walking arsenals. To judge from contemporary accounts, by late 1815 there was a greater uniformity among the cossack troops than before, some being dressed in a semi-hussar costume; but nevertheless the presence of cossacks, bashkirs, kalmucks and the like – some armed with medieval weapons and bows-and-arrows – was an incongruous feature of a 'modern' army like that of the Czar.

The Russian infantry, artillery and hussar uniform – the latter certainly one of the plainer and most handsome of the period – was completed by the uniquely-shaped 'kiwer' shako, with its strange, concave top. That shown – being examined by the cossack – is of regulation Hussar pattern. Worn exclusively by the Russian army (and a number of similar type by the Brunswick forces), the 'kiwer' was an individual head-dress, reputedly designed by the Czar himself and adopted in 1812, but was abandoned in 1815 for a bell-topped Prussian-style cap with a plate copied directly from that worn on the British 'Belgic' cap, with the British crown and cypher exchanged for the Imperial crown and the St Andrew Star. This plate (not worn by Guard regiments who retained the 'eagle' pattern) was changed in 1828 for an eagle-topped shield copied directly from the then French pattern. This plate was worn until the shako (which included coloured-cloth versions for Hussars) was replaced by the grenade-spike topped 'pickelhaube' in 1844.

5. Austria:

a) Trumpeter, 10th Hussars (Stipsicz Regt), 1815.
b) Officer, 51st Infantry (Regt Gabriel Spleny), 1815.

The traditional white uniform of the Austrian army was not worn by the army's most colourful branch, the Hussars. It was particularly apt that the Austrian army should include twelve regiments of hussars, as the term was originally applied to the Hungarian light-horsemen whose descendents served the Austro-Hungarian empire. The colourful nature of this arm can be demonstrated by the details of Austrian Hussar uniform in 1815 given in the chart.

The exact shade of the colours are as listed by Knötel. The trumpeter illustrated is taken from a contemporary print of the entry of Austrian troops into Naples in 1815. The red-faced sabretache had a border of black and yellow lace and bore a crown over the cypher F.L. in yellow.

The white infantry uniform was worn by both 'German' and 'Hungarian' units, though the Austrian regiments had rounded cuffs and white breeches, as different from the traditional Hungarian pointed cuffs and sky-blue breeches as illustrated;

Regiment	Shako	Jacket/Pelisse	Breeches	Buttons
1. Emperor Francis	black	dark blue	dark blue	yellow
2. Archduke Joseph Anton	madder red	light blue	light blue	yellow
3. Archduke Fred. Karl d'Este	ash grey	dark blue	dark blue	yellow
4. Hessen-Homburg	pale blue	parrot green	light red	white
5. Radetzky	madder red	dark green	crimson	white
6. Blankenstein	black	cornflower blue	cornflower blue	yellow
7. Liechtenstein	grass green	light blue	light blue	white
8. Elector of Hesse	black	parrot green	light red	yellow
9. Frimont	black	dark green	crimson	yellow
10. Stipsicz	grass green	light blue	light blue	yellow
11. Szekler	black	dark blue	dark blue	white
12. Palatinal	black	cornflower blue	cornflower blue	white

Hungarian regiments were further distinguished by the 'Barentatzen' lace ornament on the cuffs. In 1814 the thirteen Hungarian regiments were as listed below, together with their facing colours and their number in the Austro-Hungarian line:

2nd Alexander IV (yellow) 19th Hesse Homburg (light blue), 32nd Nikolaus Esterhazy (light blue), 33rd H. Colloredomansfeld (dark blue), 34th Paul Daidovitz (madder red), 37th Andreas Marriassy (bright red), 48th Josef Simbschen (steel green), 51st Gabriel Spleny (dark blue), 52nd Erzherzog Franz Carl (dark red), 53rd Joh. Jellachich (dark red), 60th Ignaz Gyulai (steel green), 61st St Julien (grass green), 62nd Theoror Wocquant (grass green).

Grenadiers of the Austrian army wore the famous black fur cap which has come to symbolise the Austrian forces of this period, as contemporary artists understandably illustrated it more often than the less impressive shako. The Austrian oak-leaf spray badge can be seen worn on the shako illustrated, which was frequently enclosed in a waterproof cover on active service. Despite being in close contact with the other Allied nations during the Occupation of France, Austrian uniforms changed less than those of the other great powers, the head-dress for example remaining unchanged between 1816 and 1836. Probably the Austrians realised that though their uniforms were plain in comparison to those of other nations, they were among the most handsome of all.

It should be noted that the regulations of 1811 had specified that Austrian infantry officers should have white turnbacks, but the picture on which this plate is based illustrated the unusual coloured turnbacks.

OPERATIONS IN EUROPE, 1815–1830

With the ghost of the French revolution finally laid by Napoleon's exile to St Helena, representatives of the Allied powers re-convened the Congress of Vienna, the main business of the session being to prevent, if possible, a repetition of the threat to the status quo. The impracticable and idealistic plan of Czar Alexander I to form a 'Holy Alliance' of sovereigns ruling together and assisting each other in a spirit of brotherhood was transformed by Austrian Chancellor Metternich into an enormous policing plan, whereby the allied nations would co-operate to crush any liberal movement which threatened to rock the establishment. Partly due to this, the 'long peace' which followed Waterloo was anything but peaceful.

With the exception of the Serbian Insurrection (1815–17), suppressed by Turkey, Europe was tranquil until January 1820, when part of the Spanish army mutinied at Cadiz. This grew into a full-scale revolt, led by Colonel Rafael Riego y Nunez, in which King Ferdinand VII was taken prisoner. Sparked by this revolt, the 'Oporto Revolution' in Portugal expelled the existing regency established during King John's absence in Brazil; on his return the following year, however, he accepted the insurgents' invitation to become a more constitutional monarch. More serious was General Pepe's army revolt against King Ferdinand IV in Naples; this rebellion was only quelled by the intervention of an Austrian army at the Battle of Rieti (7 March 1821). An anti-Royalist revolt in Sardinia followed, which again required Austrian assistance to help the Sardinian Royalist army gain the decisive victory at Novara (8 April 1821).

The Quadruple Alliance – Britain, Russia, Prussia and Austria – had their first real task with the revolution in Spain. At the Congress of Verona in 1822 French intervention was authorised, and in April 1823 Duke Louis d'Angoulême marched over the Pyrenees to restore the monarchy. Riego made a stand at Cadiz, but was routed by the French at the Battle of the Trocadero (31 August 1831); Ferdinand VII was freed and began to take drastic reprisals.

In 1821 began a long, bitter struggle in Greece, which aroused the most astonishing public reaction throughout Europe. Borne on a tide of romanticism which saw the Greek revolt as a crusade against the infidel, the great powers were pressured into action by tumultuous public opinion. The revolt began by a rising against the Turkish garrison in Morea, when in the 'Massacre of Tripolitsa' 10,000 Turks were slaughtered. As savage Turkish reprisals followed, all of Greece went up in flames and in January 1823 independence was declared at Epidauros. Three months later a Turkish squadron captured the island of Chios, massacring or enslaving the entire population, but lost their flagship on 18–19 June when Greek hero Constantine Kanaris sailed into the Turkish fleet with two fireships.

In July 1822 a Turkish invasion force was stopped by the fort of Missolonghi, barring the path north from the Gulf of Corinth. Investing the fort, the Turks called for reinforcements, who walked into an ambush during the night of 21 August 1822, when one Marco Bozzaris with only 300 Greeks routed the Turkish force at the Battle of Karpenizi, though at the cost of his own life. Unable to proceed, the Turks abandoned the siege of Missolonghi in January 1823, which gave the Greeks a clear chance of pressing their advantage, but this was prevented by internal dissension; it was a mistake they were to regret.

In 1825 a joint Turkish and Egyptian invasion over-ran the Morea and again laid siege to Missolonghi; for eleven months the garrison hung on until, starving, they were wiped out in a desperate final sortie. The Turks moved on to Athens, and besieged the Acropolis. By this time, however, European sympathy was fully behind the Greeks, and all manner of idealists, romantics and adventurers joined the Greek forces. The epitome of the romantic age, Lord Byron, arrived in 1822 (but died in 1824), and he was followed by militarily-experienced volunteers including General Sir George Church (given command of the Greek army) and Admiral Lord Cochrane (placed in command of the navy). Hindered by Greek inefficiency and internal strife, neither could prevent the capitulation of the Acropolis (5 June 1825), whereupon it seemed that the revolt was over. Public opinion, however, was so strong that it (among other reasons) forced the governments of Britain, Russia and France to demand the withdrawal of the Egyptian contingent and an armistice. When both were refused, the Allies sent naval forces to rendezvous off the harbour of Navarino – where lay a large Turkish fleet. Learning that the Turkish army was reputedly perpetrating atrocities ashore, the Allied commander, British Admiral Sir Edward Codrington, sailed his fleet into the midst of the Turkish ships. When a Turkish vessel fired on a British boat, the Allied fleet blasted the Turks out of existence. It virtually ended the war; the Russians took the opportunity to attack the Turks on land and gain more territory, winning important victories at Akhalzic (27 August 1828) and Kulevcha (11 June 1829); with Constantinople threatened, Turkey sued for peace and was forced to surrender the mouth of the Danube and the eastern Black Sea coast. In Greece, the Egyptian evacuation was supervised by a French expedition (early 1829), and the independent Kingdom of Greece established by the Treaty of London (1832).

Russia – ever wishing to extend her boundaries – in 1825 conducted a frontier war against Persia. After initial setbacks, General Paskievich conducted a brilliant little campaign against great odds, resulting in Persia's final destruction as a major power by the Treaty of Turkomanchi (February 1828).

More troubles flared in the Iberian peninsula; torn apart during the Napoleonic wars, bloodshed continued with a full-scale war in Portugal. King John VI's son, Miguel, attempted to re-establish an absolute monarchy, but failed in the 1823–24 Civil War. Peace was short-lived; when King John died, his heir Emperor Pedro of Brazil refused to leave South America and appointed his infant daughter to the Portuguese throne, with his youngest brother Miguel as regent. In 1826 civil war again erupted between Miguel's faction and the constitutional government, when Miguel seized Lisbon. A British expeditionary force under Sir William Clinton landed in support of General Saldhana's constitutional army, which threat compelled Miguel to relent. Clinton withdrew in April 1828, and within three months the persistent Miguel seized the throne for himself.

Supporters of the infant Queen Maria organised an army in the Azores, reinforced by British, French and Brazilian volunteers, and successfully repelled an attack by Miguel's fleet. Emperor Pedro abdicated his Brazilian throne to lead his daughter's forces, and in July 1831 France replied to Miguel's persecution of French subjects in Portugal by seizing the Miguelite fleet in the Tagus. A year later Pedro led a 'liberation' army from England which occupied Oporto, and in July 1834 British Admiral Sir Charles Napier defeated a Miguelite force off Cape St Vincent and captured Lisbon. The final act of the war occurred on 16 May 1834, when Pedro's Allied liberation army crushed Miguel's forces at Santarem; Miguel's surrender ten days later and subsequent banishment finally brought peace to Portugal.

EUROPEAN UNIFORMS 1815–1830
(PLATES 6–18)

Plates 6 to 18 illustrate the development of uniforms (principally in Britain and France where the changing of uniform-styles was most marked) during the 1815–30 period. Generally, uniforms became increasingly less functional as actual field operations (except for that part of the Russian army on their eastern frontier) were limited.

The Miguelite Wars in Portugal were an exception, with a variety of uniforms in use, basically of the traditional Portuguese style (heavily-influenced by British prototypes) with a mixture of costume brought in by the large number of foreign adventurers. The British 'Legion' – though frequently unpaid and generally maltreated by their employers – fought in an exemplary manner, being given the most desperate tasks by the Portuguese staff. Pedro's army, in fact, assumed a 'foreign legion' atmosphere: even the 'English' Queen's Lancers of General Bacon contained no less than seven nationalities! The rigours of campaigning often produced unusual 'uniforms': some of the Queen's Lancers were confined to barracks on one occasion because their costume was so ragged as to be literally indecent, while another volunteer battalion presented a most incredible sight, all the members having sworn an oath not to shave until the infant Queen was restored to her throne; the effect of three years without a haircut can be imagined!

The emergence of the Greek state in 1832 provides an example of a new army with no existing traditional uniform having to devise a regulation dress. As the new king of Greece was Prince Otto of Bavaria, it is not surprising that his army was uniformed in Bavarian style and with Bavarian assistance; infantry wore the traditional light blue jacket and trousers with red facings, with the usual 'company' distinctions – white cap-cords and wings for fusiliers, red for grenadiers, and green for rifles; bell-topped shakos were worn until the adoption of a tapering pattern in 1851. Artillery were dressed in dark blue with crimson trimming, and cavalry (as lancers) in green and crimson.

6. France:
  a) Fusilier,
     Departmental Legion,
     1816.

  b) Trooper,
     11th Chasseurs à Cheval
     (Régt de l'Isère), 1818.

Details of French infantry uniform changed a number of times after the Bourbon Restoration, with often considerable delays in the adoption of new patterns. A Bourbon shako-plate, issued to some units in the middle of 1814, was replaced upon Napoleon's return by the old Imperial pattern (where possible), which was itself replaced after Waterloo. After the second Restoration came more drastic changes – the new Royal Guard continued to wear blue, but the line regiments were completely reorganised into numbered 'Departmental Legions' each of three battalions, wearing a uniform of the 1812 pattern but in white with coloured facings, each of the eighty-six Legions having a different arrangement of the colouring on collar, lapels and cuffs. The facing colours were, for the 1st to 10th, royal blue; 11th–20th yellow, 21st 30th red, 31st–40th deep pink, 41st–50th carmine, 51st–60th orange, 61st–70th light blue, 71st–80th dark green, and 81st–86th violet. The jacket-turnbacks and shako-plumes distinguished the various companies, fusiliers having turnback-badges of the fleur-de-lys, voltigeurs of hunting-horn, chasseurs of hunting-horn and fleur-de-lys, and grenadiers of the traditional bursting grenade. Initially, the 1812 shako was worn with the 1814 Bourbon plate, but in March 1816 a narrower-topped shako was introduced, and in 1818 metal instead of white cloth cockades were adopted. A padded cloth disc was worn on fusilier shakos, of blue for the 1st battalion, red for the 2nd, and green for the 3rd (until 1819 when extra battalions were added; then the 3rd took yellow discs and the 4th green), with a brass company numeral on the disc. Grenadiers and voltigeurs had pompoms of red and yellow respectively.

Chasseur à Cheval uniform changed considerably over the years, these light cavalry troops in 1816 wearing lapelled jackets, having Hussar-style braid by 1822 and becoming single-breasted in 1831. The tall, cylindrical shakos had black plumes tipped with the facing colour, later changed to falling black plumes, though pompoms were also worn alone; in 1845 the busby was adopted at the same time as the red epaulettes (worn since 1831) were changed to white.

Under the Bourbons, regiments again assumed titles as well as numbers. Chasseur à Cheval regiments were organised in groups of three, the first in the group having both collar and collar-piping in the facing colour, the second with green collar and coloured piping, and the third with coloured collar and green piping. In 1818 regimental names and facing colours were:

1st (de l'Allier), 2nd (des Alpes) and 3rd (des Ardennes) − scarlet.
4th (de l'Ariège), 5th (du Cantal) and 6th (de la Charante) − yellow.
7th (de la Corrèze), 8th (de la Côte d'Or) and 9th (de la Dordogne) − light orange.
10th (du Gard), 11th (de l'Isère) and 12th (de la Marne) − pink.
13th (de la Meuse), 14th (du Moribhan) and 15th (de l'Oise) − carmine.
16th (de l'Orne), 17th (des Pyrénées) and 18th (de la Sarthe) − sky blue.
19th (de la Somme), 20th (du Var) and 21st (du Vaucluse) − red-violet.
22nd (de la Vendée), 23rd (de la Vienne) and 24th (des Vosges) − black.

In 1822 this scheme changed, with regiments being grouped in fours, the first two in each group having coloured collars with green piping, and the last two in each group having green collars with coloured piping. Facing colours at this time were: 1st–4th red, 5th–8th yellow, 9th–12th carmine, 13th–16th blue, 17th–20th deep pink, 21st–24th orange.

An interesting feature of the uniform illustrated − taken from a contemporary print by Canu − is the elaborate method of wearing the shako-cords.

7. **France:**
   a) **Grenadier, 7th Regt, Garde Royale (1st Swiss), Full Dress, 1817.**
   b) **Musician, 8th Regt, Garde Royale (2nd Swiss), Full Dress, 1817.**

It was traditional for the French Royal Guard to include Swiss units, these troops being ranked among the King's closest bodyguard prior to the Revolution. Upon the first Restoration, a company of 'Cent-Suisses' was established, but not revived after the Waterloo campaign. Instead, of the eight Guard infantry regiments raised upon the second Restoration, the 7th and 8th were composed of Swiss and alternatively titled the 1st and 2nd

Swiss Regiments. Unlike the other six regiments (which wore blue uniforms) the Swiss units continued to wear their traditional scarlet uniform, a colouring which had been used during the Ancien Régime and by Napoleon's Swiss corps; whereas the grenadiers of the other Royal Guard regiments wore red epaulettes (voltigeurs orange, centre companies white and chasseurs green), to prevent a clash of colour between jacket and epaulettes, the grenadiers of the Swiss regiments continued to wear the white epaulettes of Napoleon's day. All Royal Guard infantry wore the lace loops on the breast; the fur cap was reserved for grenadiers, the remainder wearing shakos.

Musicians (in every army) were traditionally distinguished by unusual costume, the most frequent variation being that the body of the uniform was of a different colour to that of the remainder of the regiment. The uniform illustrated is no exception, being in the classic 'reversed colours' style (i.e. the body of the coat in the regimental facing colour and the collar and cuffs in the usual coat-colour). An interesting feature of this uniform is the shako, being reminiscent of the Russian 'kiwer' pattern, but of a greater height. Shako-plates for musicians were frequently of a more elaborate form than those of the remainder, in this case being a representation of the Royal Arms with a trophy of flags around. The 'trefoil' epaulettes were a common musicians' distinction, dating from the Napoleonic period.

8. France:
a) Trooper, Cuirassiers of the Garde Royale, 1820.
b) Trumpeter, 3rd Dragoons, (Régt La Garonne), 1818.

In 1815 a new helmet with caterpillar crest was adopted by the French Dragoons, but was replaced by a pattern with horsehair mane authorised in July 1821; but it seems likely that in some cases it was as late as 1825 before the new pattern was issued. The green uniform-colour associated with the Napoleonic period was retained, regiments being allotted names and facing-colours in a similar style to that of the Chasseurs à Cheval, described in Plate 6. Names, numbers and facing-colours were as shown in the chart.

woven crimson ovals. The facing-colour was also borne on the shabraque.

Though Napoleon's Imperial Guard had included no cuirassiers, the Bourbon Royal Guard did; two regiments, wearing almost identical uniforms, strongly reminiscent of the cuirassiers of the Empire. The helmets were of the old pattern, but with the horsehair mane replaced by a caterpillar plume, and the cuirass emblazoned with the Royal arms. Otherwise, the costume might have belonged to a regiment of Napoleon's. Both regiments had white helmet-plumes, but the 2nd had a red ball-tuft at the base. These helmets were replaced in 1826 by a pattern lacking the skin turban, though the 2nd Regiment did not receive theirs until 1827.

Other Guard cavalry regiments also wore uniforms based upon those of their Imperial predecessors – the Dragoons had brass helmets with leopard-skin turbans, caterpillar crests and white plumes, green coatees with rose-pink facings; the Horse Grena-

---

1st (Régt du Calvados) and 2nd (du Doubs) – scarlet.
3rd (de la Garonne) and 4th (de la Gironde) – yellow.
5th (de l'Herault) and 6th (de la Loire) – light orange.
7th (de la Manche) and 8th (du Rhône) – deep pink.
9th (de la Saône) and 10th (de la Seine) – crimson.

The uniform illustrated, however, shows an interesting variation; an ornate trumpeter's uniform with yellow helmet-crest (instead of the usual black), and a blue uniform bearing regimental facings but with the musicians' lace of white with inter-

diers had fur caps with white plumes for the 1st Regiment and red-and-white for the 2nd, dark blue coats with white lace bars on the breast, with red facings for the 2nd Regiment; and the Garde du Corps a helmet similar to that of the old Gendarmes

(Plate 2), with a red-faced blue uniform, each company being distinguished in a singular manner, by coloured squares on the pouch-belt. The first four companies to be raised had white, green, blue and yellow belts respectively, and the 5th (when formed) scarlet.

9. Austria:
a) Officer, 2nd Dragoons (Regt König von Bayern), 1825.
b) Officer, Merveldt Uhlans, 1818.

Austrian uniforms changed less than those of the other four great powers, to the extent that the two illustrated are almost Napoleonic. The Austrian army contained four regiments of Uhlans (Lancers), all of whom wore a similar pattern of uniform, of green in the traditional 'lancer' style with scarlet facings and gold lace; the 3rd and 4th Regiments wore a darker shade of green than did the first two. Czapkas had cloth tops in the following colours: 1st (Merveldt) Regiment yellow, 2nd (Schwarzenberg) grass-green, 3rd (Erzherzog Karl) scarlet, 4th white. The Uhlan illustrated is taken from a watercolour by Denis Dighton; though not identified by the artist, the regiment depicted was presumably the 1st (Merveldt) from the colour of the czapka. The crimson overalls are an unusual feature, though Dighton's picture does include an officer wearing the more usual green with a double gold lace stripe down the outer seam with a red piping between the stripes. A back view in the same picture shows a most

elaborate silver-flapped pouch bearing the Imperial eagle in gilt.

The Dragoons retained the traditional white uniform with crested helmet, the head-dress remaining basically unchanged. The plain, white uniform was made even more striking by the facings, which presented a sharply-contrasting splash of colour. Facing-colours and regimental titles in 1835 were: 1st (Erzherzog Johann) black, 2nd (König von Bayern) dark blue, 3rd (Minutillo) dark red, 4th (Windisch-Graetz) light red, 5th (Eugen Prinz v. Savoyen) dark green, 6th (Ficquelmont) light blue. Buttons were white metal for all.

Austrian uniforms remained basically unchanged in style until 1849, when the tunic was adopted, though various changes had occurred before – grey trousers for 'German' regiments in 1830, altered pattern of infantry shako and light blue trousers for 'German' officers in 1836, for example. White remained the basic uniform-colour, though Uhlans and some Chevaulegers had dark green, and Hussars maintained their traditional multi-coloured garb.

10. German states:
a) Baden – Officer, Garde du Corps, 1824.
b) Hamburg – Private, Burgwehr, 1815.

This plate shows how the smaller German states copied the uniforms of larger states, both figures wearing Prussian-style uniform. The Burgwehr (Town Guard) of Hamburg wore a pattern not dissimilar from that of the Prussian Landwehr (Militia), with the low-crowned cloth shako very like the Prussian 'mütz' cap, used by regular, reserve and landwehr infantry (and some cavalry) in the Prussian army. The head-dress badge (a bugle-horn) was worn under the red and white cockade of the Hanseatic free-town forces. Officers wore silver-edged cap bands, a cockfeather plume, and a dark blue or green 'litewka' coat with green collar and pointed cuffs, both edged with silver lace, which could be used as an alternative to the 'kollet' of the other ranks. They were armed not with carbines as were the rank and file, but with curved, gilt-mounted sabres in black leather scabbards, with silver knots. N.C.O.s also had silver lace on the collar and cuffs, and white tips to the shako-plume. The hornists (buglers) had officers' pattern kollets with unlaced collar, and other ranks' shakos with a taller feather; they were armed with sword-bayonets carried from the waistbelt and used Prussianpattern 'waldhorns' with black and white cords.

The officer of the Baden Garde du Corps (from a print by J. Voellinger published in Karlsruhe in 1824) shows a typical costume of the Royal and Ducal bodyguard cavalry common throughout Germany. White uniforms for heavy cavalry – probably originating from the buff-coats worn during the seventeenth century – were the standard costume for almost all German states until the nineteenth century, some German (and Russian) units retaining them into the present century. The white uniform was equally associated with Garde du Corps units (literally, 'body-guard' cavalry), that shown (of

typical Prussian style) being adopted by the Baden Garde du Corps (raised as a palace guard in the eighteenth century) in 1819, and worn until the unit was incorporated in the Guard Dragoon Regiment in 1833. The high-crested leather helmet was equally to be found in various forms throughout Germany, Austria and Russia; in its most exaggerated forms, it reached towering – and for the wearer very precarious – heights.

11. Britain:
   a) Sergeant,
      Battalion Company,
      2nd Foot Guards, 1821.
   b) Officer,
      Grenadier Company,
      2nd Foot Guards, 1821.

This plate – based on a Denis Dighton watercolour of the 1st Battalion, 2nd (Coldstream) Foot Guards, 1821, shows the initial changes to the 'Waterloo' uniform illustrated in Plate 1. The 'Regency' shako remained unchanged, save for the removal of the back-peak which had existed on some early models, a slight increase in height, and more or less general adoption of a star-shaped plate. The short-tailed jacket was abolished for all except light troops in 1820, and in 1821 a new pattern was introduced, the officers' version having a closed 'Prussian' collar and for parade dress plastron-style lapels of the facing colour (which buttoned over to show red in undress). Breeches and long gaiters were finally discontinued in 1823, being replaced by blue-grey trousers for ordinary wear and white for parade. Fur caps for grenadier companies became obligatory for all occasions, the shakos previously worn in service dress being forbidden; but this regulation only lasted for three years.

The uniforms illustrated show not only the infantry pattern, but also the Foot Guards distinctions; the dark blue trousers worn by the officer were reserved for undress, and the sergeants' gold lace was a distinction peculiar to Guards regiments. In full dress, Guards officers wore white breeches with higher-than-knee gaiters as did the rank and file, and the full dress coatee had a red collar and was heavily-laced upon the lapels. Battalion company officers wore epaulettes instead of the wings illustrated, together with gold-laced shako with gold cords, gilt plate and chinscales, and white-over-red feather plume. Turnback-badges for the grenadier officer illustrated consisted of gold-embroidered floral sprays and bursting grenade on a blue cloth patch. Gorgets were gilt, bearing the Royal arms in silver, with blue rosettes and ribbons; these were restricted to officers in full dress. Shoulder-belt plates were also very ornate, being in the form of a silver Garter Star on a gilt plate, with blue enamel Garter and red cross. For the first time on British uniforms, the cuff-patch made its appearance on the coatees of the rank and file in this period.

12. Britain:
a) Officer, 16th Lancers, Full Dress, 1839.
b) Officer, 9th Lancers, Review Order, 1820.

At the close of the Napoleonic Wars, only Britain of the five major powers did not include regiments of lancers in her army. Those of the other nations, though having certain national characteristics, in general based their lancer uniform on the traditional Polish pattern of czapka and 'lancer' jacket. In Britain – particularly after Waterloo – public imagination was fired by both cuirassiers and lancers, probably arising from popular stories as much as from any deliberate attempt to introduce an arm which was an integral part of other armies. Though the cuirassier image had limited success (being restricted to the adoption of cuirasses by the Household Cavalry and one Yeomanry corps, the Furness Cuirassiers), that of the lancers was immediately initiated.

Lances in the British army had previously been limited to an émigré corps during the Revolutionary Wars (the Hulans Britanniques) and to that carried (unofficially) by Capt Mercer's orderly in the Royal Horse Artillery, though a scheme for raising a corps of 'British Lancers' had been suggested in 1812. In 1816, however, it was decided to convert the 9th, 12th and 23rd Light Dragoons into Lancers, the 19th Light Dragoons taking the place of the 23rd upon their disbandment after only a year.

The first uniform was based upon the 1812 Light Dragoon pattern, but with the addition of a cane-framed czapka covered with cloth of the facing colour and with a large gilt plate, 'Cossack' trousers and an abundance of lace and other adornments. There were other orders of dress, however – the Denis Dighton watercolour on which (together with a William Heath print) the 9th Lancer figure figure is based, shows an undress jacket with two vertical lines of lace down the breast, worn with grey overalls with double crimson stripe on the outer seam, and also a version with the lapels buttoned across to show a blue jacket-front. The early czapkas were usually monumental affairs, becoming smaller and less ungainly as time progressed, but those of the 9th seem always to have been better-proportioned than the bucket-shaped constructions of other regiments.

The 9th retained their crimson facings after conversion to Lancers, as did the 23rd (with silver lace); the facings of the 12th changed from yellow to scarlet, and the 16th retained their original scarlet. An 1819 print by Henry Alken shows the uniform of the 19th; their facings were light yellow and lace gold, the skulls of the officers' czapkas being literally covered with lace. Officers' girdles were gold and crimson, those of the other ranks being blue and yellow. Trousers were light blue, with a double gold stripe for officers and a single yellow one for the rank and file. Shabraques were dark blue, officers' being laced, and the other ranks' having a yellow 'vandyked' edge.

The 19th Lancers were disbanded in 1821, but the 17th Light Dragoons converted in the following year. The 1822 Dress Regulations described in detail the individual, regimental patterns of lacing on the czapka; the 17th retained their white facings. Oriental-style, 'Mameluke' swords were by this time obligatory for Lancer officers.

The 1831 Dress Regulations changed the jacket-colour from blue to red, with new blue facings and czapka-tops for all except the 17th, who kept their original white; girdles were of gold with stripes of the facing colour. Plumes were now of black cock-feathers, substituted for black horse-hair for service in India after 1834. Trousers were dark blue with double gold stripes for officers, and in 1833 gauntlets replaced the short gloves. Other ranks' sabretaches were abolished in 1834.

With the beginning of Queen Victoria's reign, all except the 16th resumed the blue jacket, with scarlet facings for the 9th and 12th, the others retaining their previous colours. The cuffs of the new uniform were pointed, and caplines were made smaller and neater from about 1846. Czapkas remained of the same pattern, though the 9th had a cap of regimental design, mainly black with gilt fittings. Officers' trousers had double gold stripes for full dress and scarlet for undress (white for the 17th), with plain white trousers for dismounted duties in summer.

The officer illustrated of the 16th – taken from a Hayes portrait of Lieut. F. Delaval Gray, from a Henry Martens portrait of Lt-Col. R. Smyth, and on a Mansion & St Eschauzier print – shows the famous red regimental uniform. It was this dress (with concessions made to tropical climates and active service such as the probable use of white cap-covers) that was worn in the regiment's immortal charge at Aliwal in the 1st Sikh War, when the 16th overran a battery of artillery, broke a 'square' of infantry and dispersed the Sikh cavalry virtually unaided – at the cost of more than a third of its strength.

13. Britain:
a) N.C.O.,
2nd Life Guards, 1833.
b) Officer,
2nd Life Guards, 1827.

Cuirasses had been worn by the Household Cavalry in the Netherlands during the Revolutionary Wars, and briefly by a subdivision of the 2nd Life Guards in 1814, but were not again used until the Prince Regent set about elaborating the uniforms of his bodyguard after Waterloo. First came a gilt-mounted steel helmet with large bearskin crest (introduced 1817) to be worn except in review order, when large, black fur grenadier caps with gilt plate, gold cords and white plume, 'three-fourths of a yard long' were to be worn.

Cuirasses, when authorised, were similar in pattern to those worn by the Household Cavalry today, except for a large gilt star-plate on the front, which was removed in about 1825. The coatee – still of scarlet with blue facings and gold lace – was long-tailed for full dress, and a shorter-tailed version existed for undress; white breeches and high boots were used for full dress, though a William Heath watercolour of c. 1820 shows the fur cap worn with what officially were undress overalls, these being of a brownish hue known as 'claret', with wide red stripes for ordinary use and gold lace stripes (for officers) for Sunday parades and special occasions. There seems to have been no rule rigidly adhered to about the wearing of the breeches or overalls – a portrait of Capt McInnes shows the full-dress breeches worn with the helmet. Sabretaches and sashes were officially laid aside in about 1829, though apparently the sashes were not worn on occasion for some years previously. A 'flask-cord' – long worn by the Royal Horse Guards – was added to the Life Guards' pouch-belts in 1829, being red for the 1st Regiment and blue for the 2nd. The Royal Horse Guards retained their dark blue uniforms with scarlet facings and gold lace, but followed the Life Guards in style; the entire Household Cavalry was issued with the cuirass for the 1821 Coronation celebrations and have worn them ever since. Undress overalls for the Royal Horse Guards were light blue, with a two-inch scarlet stripe.

The 'Roman' helmet (which had a red crest for trumpeters) was still authorised by the 1831 Regulations, but a new Grenadier cap was introduced in 1833, still with the long white plume but otherwise lighter, less ornate and minus the front plate; by this date, the Life Guards' undress trousers were dark blue with scarlet stripes. Caps of the Royal Horse Guards had red plumes.

The figure with the bearskin cap illustrated in this plate is taken from a contemporary portrait of (presumably) a senior N.C.O., which shows the pre-1833 cap probably worn in the early part of that year. This cap – which had a red cloth patch at the rear bearing an embroidered gold grenade – was a much less ornate version of that worn by the officers.

Rank-markings of the Household Cavalry are a little obscure, but the unusual inverted chevrons worn on the right arm of the figure in the portrait can only signify senior N.C.O. rank. The paintings of A. J. Dubois Drahonet are of particular value in showing the uniforms of various ranks of the Household Cavalry (and indeed the rest of the army) in about 1832.

14. Britain:
a) Sergeant, 13th Light Infantry (Summer), 1833.
b) Field Officer, 68th Light Infantry, 1829.

Uniforms of light infantry regiments followed the same general pattern as those of the line infantry, though retaining the green shako-plumes and other distinctions, including the wearing by field officers of epaulettes on top of the light infantry wings, as illustrated in the uniform of the 68th Light Infantry (taken from a portrait of [possibly] Major John Reed). When short-tailed jackets were abolished for battalion and grenadier companies in 1820, light infantry officers retained them until 1826, when the longer-tailed coatee (already used by the other ranks of light infantry corps) was adopted. From July 1830 green ball-tufts replaced the shako-plumes, and all officers and sergeants were issued with whistles, worn on the shoulder-belt, as shown in the figure of the 13th Light Infantry (taken from a portrait of Sergeant Smart by Dubois Drahonet). The white trousers shown were for summer use.

Both figures wear the new pattern

of shako authorised in 1828 to replace the 'Regency' cap, and introduced for wear in 1829, with the gold and silver lace bands (yellow or white for the rank and file) and the black cockade discontinued; the new cap was a wider-topped variety, and was worn with gold cap-lines by officers in parade or levee dress, and of white by other ranks (green for light troops). From 1829 the traditional red-and-white plumes were changed to white for all except light infantry. The plates – of very ornate design for officers and plainer styles for the men – were of a universal, crowned star shape, usually bearing the regimental number and on occasion regimental devices. This cap lasted until a changed design was introduced in 1839.

15. France:
a) Private, Marines, Undress, 1829.
b) Trooper, 8th Dragoons, 1827.

This plate illustrates the Dragoon helmet (also issued in steel to the cuirassiers) which was authorised in 1821 but in some cases probably not adopted until 1825, succeeding that shown in Plate 8. Of a most unusual pattern, of the traditional Dragoon brass, it had a horsehair mane and aigrette, and a hair 'brush' along the top of the crest. In 1826 squadron-identification in the form of a coloured ball placed at the bottom of the plume was added, in blue for the 1st squadron of every regiment, crimson for the 2nd, green for the 3rd, sky-blue for the 4th, rose-pink for the 5th and yellow for the 6th. This helmet lasted until

1840, when it was replaced by a more conventional pattern with ordinary mane and leopardskin turban. The jackets remained the traditional dragoon green in colour, but by 1823 new facing-colours had been introduced, of deep rose for the 1st–4th Regiments, 5th–8th yellow, and crimson for the 9th and 10th. Trousers were grey with piping of the facing colour, later changed to plain red for dismounted wear and red with leather reinforcing for mounted duty, but it appears that there were variations in this rule; the print from which this plate is taken shows red trousers with piping of the facing colour!

The French Marines – organised in five divisions in May 1829 – wore a most singular uniform in both full and undress. The full dress helmet was an odd-shaped item, with a spherical black leather skull and brim like a 'bowler', with a narrow brass crest supporting a black woollen crest, a brass front plate and brass bosses on the side, embossed with fleur-de-lys motif, and brass chinscales. The full dress jacket was short, of dark blue with brass buttons and shoulder-scales, worn with plain blue trousers, black gaiters and the same girdle as worn in undress. The undress uniform (chiefly remarkable for the striped cap-band and chinscales) was worn with the same equipment as full dress, having a black leather cartridge-box with brass anchor badge worn at the rear of the girdle, in the middle of the back. Bayonet and brass-hilted sword were worn in both orders of dress. The Divisions of Brest, Toulon and (until 1832) Rochefort each maintained a band, the first two of

great repute; the drum-majors' uniform included plumed busby, sash, mace, and a special pattern of sabre. The full dress helmet was abolished for wear at sea in 1832, but remained in use for shore duty until 1840.

16. France:
   **a) Officer, 8th Regt,
      Garde Royale (2nd Swiss),
      1829.**

   **b) Drum-Major, 7th Regt,
      Garde Royale (1st Swiss),
      1830.**

   **c) Bugler, Light Company,
      Infantry, 1828.**

The Departmental Legions (Plate 6) were replaced in 1822 by numbered infantry regiments in the previous manner, wearing single-breasted dark blue jackets, white trousers for summer and blue for winter, and red epaulettes for grenadiers, yellow for voltigeurs, and shoulder-straps for fusiliers. In May 1822 facing colours were allocated to all 60 regiments, a different combination of collar, cuffs, piping and turnbacks identifying the individual corps. These colours were white for regiments 1–4, 5–8 crimson, 9–12 yellow, 13–16 rose-pink, 17–20 orange, 21–24 light blue, 25–28 buff, and 29–32 green, the colour-sequence repeating from the 33rd to 60th; regiments 61 to 64 were raised in February 1823. Another new shako-plate was introduced in 1821, and a new shako in 1825, which had grenadiers and voltigeurs distinguished by double pompoms of red and yellow respectively. In 1828 facing-colours were abolished, all line regiments taking red facings, and light infantry yellow.

Musicians as usual disregarded the official regulations as shown by the bugler in this plate; in 1827 the lace chevrons on the arms were abolished, but are still worn, though the authorised collar- and cuff-lace is not; musicians of fusilier companies often wore the epaulettes and plumes officially reserved for flank companies, while in many cases drum-majors still wore the fur busby.

The two Swiss regiments of the Garde Royale illustrated show the progression in costume from those shown in Plate 7. The musicians wore 'reversed colours' of blue with red facings, the bandsmen (though not drummers and fifers attached to companies who wore the appropriate shako or grenadier cap) having busbies; the jackets, now single-breasted, retained the bars of lace on the breast. The drum major's uniform illustrated was typical of the opulent, lace-covered dress traditionally associated with French musicians.

Other Royal Guard infantry units adopted the infantry-pattern jacket in 1822, retaining their distinctive lace, and grenadiers their bearskin caps. The 1st, 2nd and 3rd Regiments had cuffs and turnbacks of crimson, rose-pink and yellow respectively, the 4th, 5th and 6th having the same facing-colour sequence but with blue cuffs, the facing colour showing on the cuff-flaps and turnbacks only. Epaulettes were white for all regiments, as were the shako- and grenadier cap-cords.

17. Netherlands:
a) Captain, 'Flanquers', 15th Infantry, 1823.
b) Trooper, 6th Hussars, 1823.

Both figures in this plate are taken from *Kleeding en Wapenrusting van de Koninklijke Nederlandsche Troepen*, published in Amsterdam in 1823, and show how the uniform of the Netherlands army – while maintaining the basic Anglo-French style worn during the Waterloo campaign – included items unique to that country.

The bell-topped infantry shako carried a unique design of plate which extended around the sides to the rear of the cap, with the regimental number embossed in large and very ornate figures on the front. As on the earlier 'Belgic' shako, the plumes of 'Flanquers' (flank companies) had coloured upper portions, with the universal orange national cockade below.

The Hussar uniform retained a very 'Napoleonic' style; trumpeters of this regiment wore red dolmans with gold lace, and black fur busbies with red bag, gold cords, gilt chinscales and a white plume rising from a gold-embroidered ball-pompom. Trumpet-cords were mixed yellow and green.

In common with the armies of many smaller European states, that of the Netherlands was expanded to include cuirassiers (previously carabiniers) and lancers in addition to the existing dragoons and hussars. Their uniforms became progressively more French in style, with wide 'cossack' trousers, metal helmets with horsehair manes, narrower-topped czapkas and (from 1849), coloured cloth French shakos for some regiments.

A squadron, later regiment, of 'Jagers te Paard' (Chasseurs à Cheval) wore a most attractive uniform in the 1843–49 period; for officers, a slightly tapering black shako with silver chinscales, dark green cock-feather plume, and silver cords and 'raquettes'; dark green short jacket with red collar and piping and silver epaulettes, dark blue trousers with red stripe, silver-laced pouchbelt with silver and gilt fittings, and a silver-laced waistbelt with red central stripe and gilt-embossed silver plate. The uniform was unchanged until the shorter, cloth shako (worn by other regiments from 1849) was introduced in 1852.

18. Papal States:
a) Trumpeter, Elite Company, 1st Regiment, Papal Carabiners, Full Dress, 1826.
b) Officer, Elite Company, 1st Regiment, Papal Carabiniers, Full Dress, 1826.

An example of Italian uniform in the early part of this period is shown by that of the Papal Carabiniers, being modelled upon Napoleonic French style. The end of French control in Italy meant that the rulers of the many small states had to re-create an army out of the organisation which remained. While attempting to eradicate many traces of Napoleonic government, a number of states established corps based upon the French Gendarmerie to act as both army and police. In the Papal States there were formed two regiments of 'Carabinieri Pontifici' in July 1815, each regiment (according to the 1816 Regulations) comprising three squadrons, each of two companies and an élite company, a total of some 76 officers and 1,746 other ranks, of whom half were mounted.

Detachments of the Carabinieri were scattered throughout the Papal States in an attempt to combat the brigandry – often approaching a full-scale guerrilla war – which plagued the rural and mountain districts and for which campaign the Pope awarded a medal (as worn by the officer in this plate). Other companies served as escort to the Pope, ranking in precedence as second only to the Noble Guard, the élite status of the corps being shown by the fact that Carabinieri officers outranked officers of similar position in the Line. Being on constant active service, the Carabinieri were the most experienced troops in the army.

Their uniform is shown in the two figures illustrated, taken from contemporary watercolours depicting the Elite Company of the 1st Regiment (the élite companies alone wore the bearskin cap, which had a red cloth patch with white grenade badge at the rear). Officers usually wore a silver aiguillette on the right shoulder; other ranks' lace was white, dismounted companies having white breeches and long black gaiters for winter, and white for summer. The bearskin was reserved for full dress, a black bicorn hat with white edging, red pompom and plume, and a Papal cockade (white with yellow edge) secured by a white loop being worn on other occasions. The brass belt-plate of the rank and file bore an embossed Papal tiara and crossed keys. In service dress a single-breasted green coatee with red collar-patches was worn, with white trousers for summer and grey-brown trousers with green stripe for winter; the greatcoat was also grey-brown with red collar-patches. N.C.O.s had aiguillettes of mixed green and silver, and silver sleeve-chevrons.

Drummers of dismounted companies wore a uniform not dissimilar from that of the privates, but the mounted trumpeters in full dress wore the magnificent costume here depicted, with the trumpet-banner bearing the regimental title, PRIMO REGGIMENTO CARABINIERI PONTIFICI. The horse-furniture of the ordinary carabiniers consisted of a white sheepskin with green 'wolf teeth' cloth edging.

In 1831 the Carabinieri participated in political riots against the Pope, and were immediately disbanded. A similar corps was later raised, which existed until 1970.

REVOLUTIONS IN EUROPE, 1830-31

The liberal political and social ideas which were by this time increasing in strength and scope were destined to cause continued conflict until the middle of the century. In Russia, officers and intellectuals, having adopted the liberal theories circulating in western Europe, formed a number of secret societies with the intention of overthrowing the still almost feudal power of the Czar. Alexander's assassination was planned for 1826, but he forestalled the plotters by dying in November 1825. The so-called 'Decembrist' revolt broke out on the day Nicholas I was proclaimed Czar, but news had been leaked of the coup and it never really got under way. Some troops (including the Moscow Guard Regiment) occupied Senate Square in St Petersburg, but were swept away with grapeshot; five of the senior plotters were executed, and the half-hearted revolt was over. It had considerable effect on the Russian army, however; Nicholas, fearful of a repetition, turned the already harsh drill into an automatic exercise to instil blind obedience into the ordinary soldier, and strangled any initiative on the part of the officers whenever it became apparent. So ridiculous did the insistence on immaculate parade-ground drill become that the infantry scarcely ever fired their muskets, which in any case were fearfully damaged by polishing with brick-dust to make them sparkle, and by loosening all the screws to make an 'attractive' rattle on parade, so that most were useless even if ammunition for target-practice had been available. Only in the Caucasus was the army kept in a state of readiness, but was regarded as unfashionable and unstylish by the remainder of the army.

In 1830 came the first serious blows to the existing order of European government, when in July the Restoration monarchy in France was toppled by a revolution in Paris. King Charles X was deposed and a new constitutional monarchy, with Charles's cousin, Louis Philippe, at its head, was established. The new régime used troops to suppress further insurrections at Lyon in 1831, and in Paris and again Lyon in 1834.

The Congress of Vienna had created a new Kingdom of the Netherlands in 1815, combining Holland, Belgium and Luxembourg under William of Orange. The association was not a happy one; Belgians resented a Protestant, and in their eyes despotic, King; and this, with the failed harvest and hard winter in 1828-30 caused the Belgian Revolution. Dutch troops were driven from Brussels in August 1830 after four days of fighting against civilians and hastily-formed volunteer units, and many Belgians serving in the Netherlands army deserted or were dismissed as being of uncertain loyalty. After a month the Netherlands army was so weak and disorganised that the Dutch National Guard had to be mobilised, and was joined by volunteer units, like those of the Belgians formed from patriotic citizens and including a number of rifle corps raised from university students. In October Belgian independence was declared, and in the same month General Chassé, occupying the Antwerp citadel for the King, strengthened anti-Dutch feeling by his bombardment of the city.

The danger of a European war of large proportions loomed. The new French government prepared an army to help in the 'liberation' of Belgium, and many Belgians favoured a union with France. Prussia, Austria and Russia were prepared to help Holland. A conference of the great powers called in London agreed upon a temporary armistice in November, and decided in the following month, thanks to the efforts of Metternich and the Duke of Wellington (later Palmerston after Wellington's government fell), that the Kingdom of the Netherlands should be dissolved, with Belgium becoming an independent, neutral state whose independence was guaranteed by the major powers. In June 1831, after a search for a King that at times approached sheer farce, Leopold of Saxe-Coburg was 'elected' King Leopold I of Belgium.

Leopold requested – and got – Luxembourg as part of his new kingdom. This prompted King William of Holland, who had watched the political manoeuvring with increasing anger, to act on his own. Commanded by Crown Prince William (the somewhat incompetent veteran of Waterloo), a Dutch field army of some 50,000 men marched over the border in three columns, intending to divide the two hastily-assembled, volunteer Belgian armies facing them. Both sides included volunteer and National Guard units, which performed with credit at the Battle of Hasselt (7 August 1831). The outcome was that the Belgian Army of the Meuse fell back on Liège in disorder. The Dutch then turned to face the Belgian Army of the Scheldt, falling back upon Brussels. With many of the Army of the Meuse's volunteer units demoralised and disintegrating, Belgian fortunes were desperate; they were saved, however, by a French army of 60,000 under Marshal Gérard who marched into Belgium on 8 August. Assured by the French government that they would withdraw as soon as hostilities ceased, the other major powers agreed that they were acting in the interests of the London Conference.

Marching on Louvain, the Dutch met stiff resistance, particularly from the Brussels 'Gardes Civique', but by 12 August the Army of the Scheldt was almost surrounded in Louvain. On receiving news that both Britain and France demanded an armistice, with a British fleet sailing to blockade Dutch ports and Gérard's army coming up quickly, the Crown Prince decided it prudent to withdraw. Though the war was virtually over, Chassé was still besieged in Antwerp (this time by the French) which he held until 1832. A formal armistice was concluded in May 1833, but only in April 1839 was the independence of Belgium recognised by the Dutch.

The Belgian Revolution is the best-known of the 1830 revolts, but an even more serious insurrection occurred in Poland, and this time there was no intervention from the major powers as there had been to save Belgium. The Congress of Vienna had once more divided Poland (as the Duchy of Warsaw) between Prussia, Austria and Russia. The Russian piece became the 'Congress Kingdom', with the Czar ruling as King of Poland.

The Poles' characteristic hatred of foreign domination erupted into insurrection in Warsaw in November 1830, following recurrent friction with the Russians in previous years. The Polish revolt began when it did partly as a result of the Belgian rebellion; while giving the Belgians moral support the Poles feared that the Czar might use the Polish army to assist the Dutch, but when Belgian success became apparent the Poles decided upon an attempt to throw off the repressive Czarist régime which had deprived them of numerous democratic rights.

The Polish army – Russianised almost completely – was only some 30,000 strong, but expanded at an incredible rate as volunteers flocked to join hastily-raised corps, until over 80,000 men were in the field. Beginning in Warsaw – where the patriots became over-enthusiastic and massacred Russian-supporters – the revolt spread and an element of anarchy ensued. Not only did the Poles claim to be merely asserting their rights, but they also called for the deposition of the Czar. This, coupled with the great bloodshed and the fact that both Austria and Prussia had Polish subjects who might rise if the Polish revolt went against Russia, inevitably resulted in Polish appeals for help going unheeded.

Russian generals Diebitsch and Paskievich with 114,000 men brought fire and sword to the area, whilst Polish factions fought each other for supremacy. At the Battle of Grochkow (20 February 1831), however, a Polish army under Prince Radziwell halted Diebitsch in a sanguinary fight. On 26 May Diebitsch was again engaged, this time by Polish general Skrzneki, in the long and fearfully bloody Battle of Ostrolenka, an indecisive fight which nevertheless caused Skrzneki's withdrawal. The Poles, now commanded by General Dembinski, retired to Warsaw, which Paskievich stormed on 6–8 September 1831. After a gallant defence, the Russian capture of the city was accompanied by the most horrific slaughter, and the insurrection extinguished in an extremely violent manner.

The revolutions of 1830—31 (which also included revolts in Modena, Parma and the Papal States, largely inspired by Guiseppe Mazzini and only suppressed with Austrian assistance) had little effect on the military costume of the large states, but produced in both Belgium and Poland a style of dress which was to become politically-identifiable with republicans, democrats and adherents of other predominantly proletarian movements, a uniform based upon working-clothes and smocks, though of a necessarily ornate form to conform to established military tenets. This style of uniform was due to appear again throughout Europe, later including politically-styled felt hats and 'democratic' haircuts!

European Uniforms 1830-31 Plates (19-22)

19. **Holland:**
   a) **Drummer,**
      Guard Grenadiers,
      Full Dress, 1831.
   b) **Private,**
      Flanquers, 8th Infantry,
      Full Dress, 1831.

The standard Dutch infantry uniform consisted of bell-topped shako with the usual orange cockade, gilt plate of 'sunburst' shape with white metal number, and red pompom (green for 'flanquer' companies). On active service (such as the invasion of Belgium) the shako was covered with a black 'waterproof' bearing the regimental number in white paint. The uniform was as illustrated for all regiments, except that only the 'flanquers' wore wings, the remainder having white-edged blue shoulder-straps. The grey trousers were officially worn in winter with grey gaiters, both items being white for summer, the fashion illustrated being a combination of the two. Greatcoats were double-breasted, of medium grey, with brass buttons and white collar-patches.

Grenadiers wore a similar uniform, but with large fur cap, which had a patch on the back bearing a white grenade. Grenadier 'flanquers' wore the infantry shako with green pompom and red tuft, and a grenade on the plate, with white grenade painted on the shako-cover. Grenadiers also wore red wings and facings, yellow lace loops, white shoulder-straps piped red with brass grenade badges, white grenades on the turnbacks and red-laced greatcoat-collars.

Light Infantry wore regulation shakos with brass regimental number and hunting-horn badge and green pompom, with white hunting-horns on the covers; double-breasted green jackets with yellow piping, dark green wings, and yellow hunting-horn turn-back badges; greatcoat as before but with yellow-laced collar.

The universal infantry equipment consisted of pack, linen haversack, iron mess-tin and canteen, and black leather cartridge-box bearing a grenade or hunting-horn where appropriate; N.C.O.s and musicians carried short swords in addition to the usual bayonet, which was often fastened to the side of the cartridge-box. Sword-knots were of white and orange (green for light infantry). Officers wore gold lace epaulettes, with thin fringes for company officers and bullion fringes for those of field rank, the epaulettes of 2nd Lieutenant and Major having two silver stripes on the strap, and those of 1st Lieutenant and Lieutenant-Colonel one silver stripe. Adjutants wore fringeless epaulettes, corporals two yellow lace chevrons, sergeants one gold chevron, and sergeant-majors two gold chevrons.

20. **Belgium:**
    a) **Officer,**
       Tirailleurs Liègois
       (Luikse Tirailleurs),
       1830.
    b) **Officer,**
       Civil Guard, 1831.

c) **Private,**
   Bataillon de l'Escaut
   (Bataljon van de Schelde),
   1837.

This plate shows the evolution of Belgian rifle uniform (most of the hastily-raised volunteers being light infantry or riflemen), and the Civil Guard dress.

The Tirailleurs Liègois wore a typically-French style uniform, though of the unusual brown colour, recalling the famous Portuguese Caça-dore colours of the Peninsular War. Other details – pattern of shako, cut of the uniform, even the gorget – are all obviously French in design. The Civil Guard uniform is the classic 'smock-frock' garment inspired by civilian working clothes, at once both politically significant and (much more important in times of emergency) easily produced. It was also one of the most comfortable, serviceable garments yet designed. The contemporary print upon which this figure is based also shows certain concessions to current military fashion – aiguil-lettes for musicians and fur busbies for pioneers, for example. The shako, of French style, bears the new Belgian cockade of red, yellow and black.

Jackets or long, litewka-style garments were also much-favoured by the Belgian volunteers, frequently worn with 'round hats' of felt or leather, generally resembling a tall 'topper' with one side of the brim turned up. One 1831 corps, for example, the Partisans of Capiaumont, wore green knee-length coats with red piping, grey trousers, and black hats with red cap-lines, national cockade and pom-poms of the national colours, from which rose a 'falling' plume of black horsehair. Cartridge-boxes were often worn at the front of the waist-belt, and often bore a hunting-horn device. A progression from the early volunteer uniform can be seen in the dress of the Batallion de l'Escaut in 1837, which while retaining the essential character of volunteer uniform has become more of an issue dress and less of an emergency measure like that of the Civil Guard.

21. Poland:

a) Voltigeur, 4th Infantry Regt, 1826.

b) Officer, 1st Lancers, 1830.

This plate shows the uniform of the Polish army prior to the 1830–31 revolution. While maintaining traditional Polish elements (for example the lancer uniform) the style was copied directly from that of Russia. With the exception that all Polish infantry wore coloured lapels (only the Russian Guards did), the general pattern was almost identical; even the enormous, thin plume characteristic of Russian infantry shakos was used by some Polish corps. Some independence was maintained, however, in the Polish helmet-plate worn on both the shako and czapka. Horse Artillery wore a dark green uniform with black facings and red piping, reminiscent of that of the Duchy of Warsaw, the colouring of the uniform being the only relic of Polish participation in Napoleon's army.

22. Poland:

a) Sandomir Volunteers, 1830–31.

b) Podlasie Volunteers, 1830–31.

This plate illustrates two of the exotic uniforms worn by volunteer units during the 1830–31 revolution, taken from a contemporary print. The knee-length frock-coat was extensively used, coupling traditional Polish features with the more 'romantic' style favoured throughout Europe. Grotthus' Sandomir Volunteers were dressed in a 'grenadier' style with eagle-plated bearskin cap, while Colonel Kuszell's Podlasie Volunteers wore the old 'Konfederatka' head-dress, a Polish cap which was the forerunner of the czapka. Both these figures are taken directly from a contemporary picture, and the colouring reproduced exactly; it is interesting to note, however, that Knötel's *Handbuch der Uniformkunde* gives both the coat of the Sandomir corps and the facings of the Podlasie as green. On the cap of the Podlasie Volunteers was borne the traditional Polish Maltese Cross device, over a skull and crossed bones, signifying the genuine determination of the Polish patriot army.

The Konfederatka was also worn by two of the regular infantry units raised in 1830–31; that of the 10th Regiment, for example, had a scarlet cloth top with lower band of white fur, with silver-laced cockade and white upright plume (for officers), worn with a full-skirted blue coat with scarlet collar, cuffs, lining and piping, dark blue trousers with red stripe, silver epaulettes and laced belts.

One of the most unusual uniforms was that of the 'Krakus', a corps bearing the same name as that of Napoleon's army (named from the town of Cracow). They wore crimson-topped Konfederatkas with black fur band and green plume, cream-coloured knee-length coat with crimson collar, pointed cuffs and cartridge-tube-pockets on the breast (as in Plate 32), grey trousers with double crimson stripes, with long green greatcoats with attached cape, lined crimson and with collar and cuffs of the same, and much silver lace around the bottom edge of both coat and cape; the corps was armed with sabre (supported by a black waistbelt) and lance with crimson-over-white pennon. Other volunteer cavalry adopted black uniforms; the Kalisch Volunteer Lancers, for example, had black coats with sky-blue facings, crimson girdles, black trousers with sky-blue stripes, sky-blue czapka-tops and crimson over sky-blue lance-pennons. National Guard units generally wore dark blue coats, trousers and Konfederatkas with red facings and black equipment.

OPERATIONS IN EUROPE, 1830–40

Trouble in Italy continued, still stirred up by Mazzini, and still foreign assistance was required to hold the rebellions in check; Austrian troops occupied Romagna (January 1832) and French troops took Ancona in March. A Mazzini uprising in Piedmont and Savoy failed in 1834 causing one of his supporters, a young Sardinian sailor named Garibaldi, to flee for his life. Sporadic insurrections continued to flare up for years. Intervention in the affairs of minor states by established powers was not limited to Italy, however; in 1832 a Bavarian expeditionary force went to assist King Otto of Greece in retaining his power, and remained there until 1837.

Russia's expansionist policy kept her frontier armies constantly active, thus preventing the whole of the Russian army from becoming bogged down in a mire of parade-ground precision at the expense of efficiency. After the 1828–29 war against Turkey (ostensibly to support Greece but actually to further their own aims) they became involved in the First Turko–Egyptian War of 1832–33, by assisting Turkey to resist an Egyptian attack! When a Russian squadron arrived at Constantinople, both England and France were sufficiently afraid of the extension of Russian influence that they arranged a peace by the Convention of Kutahia. It was not the first time since 1815 that these two nations had concerned themselves with oriental affairs; in 1816 an Anglo–Dutch fleet under British Admiral Lord Exmouth (Edward Pellew) destroyed the Algerian fleet in Algiers harbour to discourage piracy, and British demonstrations were again necessary in 1819, a further bombardment of Algiers in 1824, and a French blockade of the port in 1827–29.

Pushing onwards, Russian forces moved into Turkestan. Advancing into the Khanate of Kiva, General Perovsky's expedition ended in disaster (1839); thereafter, the Russians moved more slowly until completing the task in 1847.

The main theatre of war during this period, however, was in Spain. Ferdinand VII, before his death in 1833, nominated his infant daughter Isabella to reign under the regency of his wife, Maria Christina, instead of passing the throne under Salic law to his brother, Don Carlos. As soon as Ferdinand died, Carlos organised a revolt to take the throne for himself; Britain, France and Portugal all entered into an alliance with the Spanish government to help in the rebellion's suppression. From Britain went the 10,000 strong 'British Legion', a mercenary body recruited under the authority of Parliament and commanded by Sir George de Lacy Evans. Of the 10,000 troops, Evans himself admitted that about 2,200 were so infirm or old as to be unfit for service. Many Peninsular War veterans were included in its ranks, including the well-known soldier–author Edward Costello, a sergeant of rifles in the Peninsular War but a light infantry captain in the Legion. France 'rented' her entire Foreign Legion to Spain, this élite corps forming the nucleus of the badly-led loyalist army. In five years of ferocious guerrilla war of almost unparalleled savagery, the Foreign Legion was all but destroyed, though winning themselves a great reputation at Terapegui (26 April 1836) and Huesca (24 March 1837). When the bitter war was concluded by the Confederation of Vergara (31 August 1837), the defeated Don Carlos took refuge in France.

Apart from the uniforms (or in some cases lack of them) worn by the armies involved in the Carlist War, there was insufficient 'active service' in Europe in the 1830–40 period to impose any check upon the development of military costume. Only in the uniforms shown in Plates 38 and 39 was any real concession made to efficiency rather than 'show'; towards the end of the 1830's, however, signs of a gradual simplification were beginning to appear in some cases, though this had little effect on the ornate character of uniforms in general.

EUROPEAN UNIFORMS 1830–40 (Plates 23–39)

23. Britain:
  **a) Bandmaster,
     Royal Marines, 1823.**
  **b) Officer,
     Royal Marine Artillery,
     1840.**

The Royal Marines were organised in battalions of infantry and batteries of Royal Marine Artillery. One battalion and one battery accompanied the British Legion in the Carlist War, greatly distinguishing themselves at the Battle of Hernani in 1837. Otherwise, their service during this period was limited to small expeditions in the Mediterranean and oriental sphere of operations.

Marine uniforms followed the respective infantry and Royal Artillery styles, with regimental badges and distinctions. The artillery officer illustrated wears what was basically the dress worn in Spain, except for slight alterations in the shako caused by the 1839 Regulations. While conforming to Royal Artillery style, the traditional Royal Marine emblems were worn as badges – an anchor on the shako-plate, a lion and crown and a bursting grenade (the latter to indicate the artillery rôle) on the belt-plate. In 1827 King George IV directed that, in view of the services of the Royal Marines in every corner of the world, they should be granted as a badge 'the Great Globe itself', which emblem is proudly used by the corps to this day.

Other ranks' uniforms of the artillery were similar to those of the officers but minus the lace, and with brass shoulder-scales and white ball-tufts on the shakos. A painting of the Battle of Hernani shows this uniform in use, with officers wearing undress caps and frock-coats instead of the uniform illustrated. The infantry battalions wore red uniforms with blue facings, but like their counter-parts in the Line, the musicians were uniformed in a most exotic manner. The drum-major wore a more or less regulation dress – red faced blue – with the requisite yards of gold lace, a drooping white horsehair plume on the shako, and light blue trousers; other bandsmen, however, wore the uniform as shown on the illustration of the bandmaster in this plate, taken from a picture by E. Hull. The white uniform (much favoured by infantry bandsmen), the addition of red plume and trousers, together with much gold lace, made the uniform one of the most attractive of the army.

24. Britain:
a) Sergeant,
   14th Light Dragoons, 1832.
b) Officer,
   3rd Foot Guards, 1832.

The reign of William IV saw the infantry uniform change very little, the most notable feature being the adoption by the 2nd and 3rd Foot Guards of a uniform to match that of the 1st, by the introduction of the bearskin cap previously the unique distinction of the Grenadier Guards. By 1831 it was intended to re-name the other two regiments to increase their prestige, and alter their dress to fusilier pattern; in the event, although both took the fur cap, the 2nd Cold-stream Guards name was retained and only the 3rd Regiment became the Scots Fusilier Guards. The fur caps had front plates in the design of a crowned Tudor rose, frequently half-hidden by fur. Caps of officers of the Scots had a small gilt Star of the Order of the Thistle on the back of the cap. The uniform illustrated (from a portrait of Lieutenant & Captain the Hon. H. Montagu by A. J. Dubois Drahonet) included the white plume initially taken by all three regiments, though eventually the Scots dis-carded theirs and the Coldstreams took a red plume on the right-hand side of the cap instead. An interesting feature of the uniform illustrated was the collar, only the front half of which was in the blue facing-colour, the rear portion being red. The officers' collar-badge was the Star of the Order of the Thistle.

By 1822 there remained only five light dragoon regiments, the 3rd, 4th, 11th, 13th and 14th, wearing a blue uniform similar to that of the 1812 pattern, with heavily-laced shako and (from 1822) drooping red and white plume (of feathers for officers). The 3rd had scarlet facings, the 4th light yellow, the 11th and 13th buff and the 14th orange; trousers were sky-blue in the 1822 Regulations and blue-grey in those of 1828. Musicians (frequently negroes) often wore white uniforms; those of the 4th in 1822, for example, according to a painting by J. Pardon, wore white jackets with red facings, red trousers with white stripe, and red cloth shakos with white lace and red-and-white plume.

William IV attempted to clothe the entire army in red, and enjoyed some success; the light dragoons took red jackets in about 1832, following instructions to do so in 1831. The 3rd and 14th took blue facings, the 4th yellow (changed to green in 1836), and the 11th and 13th continued to wear buff, that of the 13th being so pale as to be almost white. Only the officers of the 3rd and 13th had previously worn gold lace (yellow for the other ranks), but all regular officers were ordered to wear gold lace in 1830, silver being reserved for the militia. Jackets remained double-breasted but lost the coloured lapels; girdles were (for officers) of gold lace with two coloured stripes, crimson being the colour according to the 1834 Regulations. The bell-topped shako was heavily-laced and had a Maltese Cross plate; officers' plumes were supposedly of white feathers but in some cases the red-and-white style continued. Horsehair plumes were worn by some officers as well as by the other ranks. The figure illustrated shows the regulation uniform of the 14th, based upon a Dubois Drahonet portrait of Sergeant John Brookfield. Most notable is the blue-striped girdle, not changed (officially) until

1834. The black leather sabretache bore a brass badge in the shape of a crowned Maltese Cross, as on the shako.

25. Britain:
   a) Officer, Royal Artillery, Undress, 1828.
   b) Officer, Battalion Company, 15th Foot, 1832.
   c) Sergeant, Light Company, 46th Foot, Undress, 1837.

The 1828–29 shako has already been described (Plate 14). The officer of the 15th (East Yorkshire) Regiment (taken from a contemporary print) shows the change in infantry dress from the post-Waterloo style; prior to 1829 officers' undress jackets had buttoned-over lapels, hiding the panel of the facing colour, but in that year the coloured lapels were abolished completely. From 1826, other ranks' jackets were altered by the addition of a lace loop on the collar, and the loops on the breast changed to decrease in length nearer the waist. From 1835 the tall plume was replaced by a white ball-tuft. As already mentioned, all regular officers wore gold lace from 1830, and the gorget was finally abandoned. Regimentally-patterned lace for other ranks was discontinued in favour of plain white in 1836, in which year sergeants adopted un-laced, officer-style coatees. In 1833 winter trousers were ordered to be grey, with a red stripe on the outer seam; white trousers were still used for summer.

In the 1840's infantry uniforms at last began to change for the better, though even at the beginning of the

Crimean War were still no more functional than they had been in 1815. A simpler pattern of fur cap was adopted by the Guards in 1835, and all ranks were given epaulettes (white for the rank and file). A new shako was authorised in 1839; still bell-topped, it had a leather chinstrap (later a chain) instead of scales, other ranks' plates being in the form of a crowned disc bearing the regimental number; from 1843 ball-tufts were red and white for battalion companies. In 1844 the 'Albert' shako, of 'stovepipe' form (see Plate 28) replaced the bell-topped cap, copied probably from Austro-French designs. From 1845 sergeants' sashes no longer carried stripes of the facing colour, and in 1848 the false pockets were removed from the coat-tails. The white summer trousers, though still worn in the colonies, were deemed to cause rheumatism at home, and were replaced in 1846 by a lavender-coloured cloth which faded rapidly and was itself replaced by dark blue in 1850. Grenadier caps were discontinued in 1842 for the shako with white ball-tuft, also worn by Fusilier regiments; on the 'Albert' cap these were also worn, Fusiliers having grenade-shaped plates instead of the usual star, though the 5th Fusiliers wore a half-red, half-white ball-tuft. Light infantry corps had green ball-tufts, and by this time the strange habit of wearing both epaulettes and wings had lapsed, field officers of all infantry wearing epaulettes alone.

The Royal Artillery officer (taken from a print by E. Hull) shows the plain, undress uniform with unlaced frock-coat adopted by the Royal Artillery in about 1828; from 1834 it was worn with blue cloth fringeless epaulettes, and from 1838 with red piping and gilt shoulder-scales. The undress cap was an oilskin-covered cane construction like the ordinary shako in shape, without any decorations at all; from 1833 a blue cloth cap, gold-laced and with a leather peak, was the regulation 'forage cap'.

Infantry undress is shown by the sergeant of the 46th (South Devonshire) Regiment, taken from a watercolour by M. A. Hayes. Battalion companies wore white shoulder-straps in place of wings on the unlaced undress jacket, and the peaked cap (here covered by a 'waterproof') was reserved for sergeants, other ranks having a blue woollen 'pillbox'-type cap without peak, with a white pompom in the centre of the crown (red for the light company, a regimental distinction of the 46th), with brass numerals '46' on the front (with a brass bugle-horn for the light company). This regiment had a most spectacular band uniform at this date – drummers wore shakos with red ball-tuft but no cords, and tail-less white jackets with red collar and pointed cuffs, red wings and red hussar-style braiding; musicians had shakos with drooping white horsehair plumes, white shako-cords on the front, with black falling cords and 'raquettes', long-tailed white coats with white lapels, yellow collar, round cuffs and turnbacks; both wore dark blue trousers with a wide red stripe, and carried brass, 'mameluke' – hilted swords.

26. Britain:
a) Trumpeter, 11th Hussars, Marching Order, 1845.
b) Officer, 10th Hussars, Full Dress, 1833.

Hussar uniform, traditionally the most elaborate of all, went through a series of dazzling changes which it is impossible to list comprehensively here. Briefly, in 1819 only the 18th Hussars still wore the busby, the others having shakos – light blue for the 7th, black for the 10th and red for the 15th. The 18th, however, were disbanded and their place taken by the 8th Light Dragoons, converted to Hussars in 1822. The shako, now universal, was bell-topped, all except the 7th adopting a lower pattern in 1828. In 1822 the closed, 'Prussian' collar was taken into use on the dolman, which had a profusion of lace, silver for the 8th and 15th and gold for the others. Pelisse-fur was white for the 10th, black for the 15th and grey for the others. The 8th, when converted, took tall black shakos with green feather plumes (for officers). Trousers were blue for the 7th, dark grey with red stripes for the 8th and scarlet for the others, with gold or silver lace stripes for officers. Facing-colours were (as in 1815) white for the 7th, red for the 15th and dark blue for the others, though for a time the 8th retained their red-faced sabre-taches (this being their facing - colour as Light Dragoons). In 1823 blue-grey overalls were ordered for all the cavalry, but the 15th retained their regimental dark grey pattern. As hussar dress became more elaborate, the prices of uniforms meant that only the richest officers could afford to belong to a hussar regiment; whereas in 1829 an infantry officer's uniform cost £40, that of the 10th Hussars cost no less than £399–7s.–6d.!

William IV's desire to re-clothe the army in red was resisted by the hussars, who only adopted red pelisses (all with black fur). The 8th and 15th, previously wearing silver, adopted the gold lace ordered in 1830 about a year later. The 7th still retained their tall cap, and the 15th their distinctive red shako; from 1831 all wore dark blue overalls with gold lace stripe (yellow for other ranks). Shabraques were perhaps the most elaborate part of an ornate ensemble at this time, as can be seen from the uniform illustrated, taken from a Mansion & St Eschauzier print.

In the 1840's the general trend towards simplification affected even Hussar regiments, without fundamentally altering their magnificent appearance. In 1840 the 11th Light Dragoons were converted to Hussars, taking fur caps, the usual dolman and pelisse, and the most distinctive crimson trousers. After the 11th had resurrected the busby, the other regiments followed suit, these being officially ordered for all Hussars in 1841, all of the same pattern – brown fur with red bags (crimson for the 11th), white-over-red plumes, gold cap-lines (yellow for the rank and file) encircling the cap and joining the bag, and falling as long cords and 'raquettes'. There was some reticence to abandon the more decorative shako – the 15th, in fact, retained their jealously-guarded scarlet caps until 1856 – and the 10th wore the shako in undress, unofficially until receiving official permission in 1846. The 10th and 11th were permitted double lace stripes on their trouser-seams. Shabraques remained ornate, dark blue for the 7th and 8th, crimson for the 11th and scarlet for the others.

An interesting version of the hussar uniform is shown in the 11th Hussars trumpeter in this plate, taken from a M. A. Hayes print illustrating marching order. The pelisse is worn as a jacket, and the distinctive crimson overalls are retained, but the uniform has an otherwise plain aspect befitting field service. The fur cap (with plume removed) is nonetheless most striking, being of the white fur pattern reserved for regimental trumpeters. Unusually, the original print shows the trumpet without any cords.

27. Britain:
a) Officer, Worcestershire Yeomanry, 1834.
b) Officer, West Somerset Yeomanry, 1846.

Like other European nations, Britain experienced civil disturbance in the years following Waterloo, which kept army detachments fully occupied on 'internal security' operations. In this, regulars were assisted by the militia and (more usually) the yeomanry, a mounted volunteer cavalry force. Originally raised in the 1790's, the yeomanry fulfilled the duties of both an internal defence force to resist foreign invasion and as a type of mobile police force, ready to be called upon to suppress riot or insurrection whenever it occurred.

Yeomanry uniforms varied greatly during this period, with numerous unique patterns in use; many, however, styled their dress upon current light dragoon costume. For example, that of the Worcestershire Yeomanry illustrated (from a Richard Dighton watercolour) included the bell-topped shako and double-breasted jacket, but when compared to the regulation light dragoon costume (Plate 24) the differences are obvious. The chinscales were purely decorative as a leather chinstrap was always used; a regimental distinction was the black rosette worn under the plume-socket, fastened by a metal crown. Another Dighton picture of 1832 shows this uniform again, but with other ranks depicted; a trumpeter, for example, wears substantially the same uniform but with a red plume and large red woollen wings in place of epaulettes. Farriers wore black plumes and dark blue jackets faced buff, with a white inverted horseshoe badge on the right upper arm; they were armed with large axes. The Worcestershires included a horse artillery troop, also wearing black plumes, but with red facings to their blue jackets. Shabraques were of great simplicity – dark blue, pointed-ended, with a white lace border and no decoration. Regimental facings changed to blue in 1850 when the regiment was granted the title 'Royal'.

The West Somerset wore a more regulation light dragoon style. The blue jacket was introduced for regular light dragoons in 1840, when the remaining four regiments again changed their facing-colours: scarlet for the 3rd, 4th and 14th and buff for the 13th, borne on the collar, cuffs and turnbacks. Trousers were dark blue with a double gold lace stripe for officers on dress occasions, red for other ranks and officers' undress (buff stripes for the 13th). The shako, as described by the 1846 Regulations, resembled the infantry cap in shape, gold-laced for officers and retaining the Maltese Cross shaped plate; officers' plumes were of white swan-feathers, but horsehair plumes like those of the rank and file were used for service in India. On service, other ranks' shakos were covered in black oilskin, but officers had oilskin-covered, light cane caps of the same shape as their 'foul weather' head-gear. The West Somerset uniform (taken from a Henry Martens water-colour) is based upon this pattern, though regimental devices could be seen in the interlaced WSY cypher on the sabretache and shabraque, the former having a blue cloth ground and gold lace edge.

The yeomanry supplied many useful services during this period of civil unrest, some corps becoming thoroughly hated by certain elements of society as a result. Frequently the yeomanry were set upon by rebellious mobs who would not have dared to treat regular cavalry in such a manner, as the part-time soldiers were in many cases more reticent about using force on their fellow-countrymen (the over-propagandised 'Peterloo' incident notwithstanding), and the yeomen, in defending themselves, often caused considerable bloodshed. A typical 'internal security' incident (which could have occurred in almost any country in Europe) was recorded by Lieutenant Charles Loftus of the

Raynham Troop of Norfolk Yeomanry, called out in June 1835 to suppress a serious disturbance and house-burning at Docking. The severity of the outbreak can be judged from a note in the *Norfolk Chronicle* of 29 June, describing 'eight or nine hundred ill disposed persons, all armed with deadly clubs'. Loftus received the alarm at 11 p.m., sent out riders from his house, and by six o'clock the following morning not only was his own troop assembled in marching order, but the Dereham troop also.

Arriving in the troubled area, the Yeomen (commanded by Major the Hon. J. G. Milles) found the local coast-guards barely able to keep the streets quiet. Deciding on a show of force, Milles marched his men into Docking, 'drawing up in front of the inn, where we halted two hours, so many men dismounting at a time to get refreshment. Our appearance had a good effect, for men who were standing about in groups, talking of . . . riot and planning mischief, dispersed almost at once . . . We got some cold beef and sandwiches, a provision with which we were satisfied. Major Milles slept that night by the side of his horse, as he did at Quatre Bras. Everything passed off quietly. The labourers who had created this disturbance were wonderfully surprised when they saw the soldiers coming, and so promptly, too, from far and wide, and would not believe that they were Yeomanry Cavalry, but the Dragoons from Norwich, our dress being that of heavy Dragoons, and completely deceived the yokels. At noon on the following day a troop of 17th Lancers came from Norwich, and our corps marched home . . . '.

That was one incident when good sense prevailed, aided to no little extent by the uniform of the Norfolk Yeomanry, making the potential rioters think that they would be opposed by the tougher regular cavalry with less scruples about cutting down a few dissidents as an example to the remainder. Tragically, other incidents culminated in violence and bloodshed, though it is certain that the existence of an active force of yeomanry prevented far greater loss of life and property than that at times occasioned by their presence.

Sadly, the yeomanry were not always appreciated: a regular dragoon officer, for example, wrote to the *United Services Journal* in January 1834 to complain at the presence of a yeomanry officer observer at the Austrian army manoeuvres in Lombardy in 1833, saying that he could see no reason for the yeoman's presence, as he would probably not learn anything of use and considered it only an excuse to display his 'provincial uniform'. And a northern newspaper in 1827, in typical miserly and ungrateful fashion, wrote that 'We find the Yeomanry cost us for 48 days service £29,949, that is, we pay this sum for 360 gentlemen amusing themselves . . . '.

28. Britain:
a) Officer, 6oth King's Royal Rifle Corps, 1833.
b) Private, Rifle Brigade, 1849.
Rifle corps retained their unique 'rifle-green' colouring made famous by the Peninsular and Waterloo campaigns, though following the general infantry style. Until 1816 they used the old 'stovepipe' shako, then adopted the 'Regency' cap and (for a time) light blue overalls for officers cut in cossack style and copied from Russia. Until 1820, the 2nd Battalion of the 6oth (Royal American) Regiment was dressed as light infantry, but became 'rifles' in that year; the 95th Rifles were taken out of the numbered sequence of regiments as an added distinction, henceforth known as The Rifle Brigade.

The 1822 Regulations confirmed the hussar-style uniform of both corps, including pelisse with black fur (for officers) and black ball-tuft on the cap, with red facings for the 6oth (named the Duke of York's Own in 1824) and black for the Rifle Brigade; green cock-tail plumes were authorised for officers in 1824, and greatcoats (hitherto blue) were changed to the distinctive green. Other ranks had three rows of buttons on the breast, and black-laced collar and cuffs. In 1833 the 6oth became the King's Royal Rifle Corps; the ball-tuft was resumed on the shako (which had bronzed fittings) and in 1833 black buttons replaced the previous white metal variety. In 1834 the cap-lines and large shako plate were discontinued, and the Rifle Brigade clothed entirely in green, with only the crimson girdle and mounted officers' black pelisse to add a touch of colour. The 'Albert' cap was adopted by rifle units at the same time as the remainder of the army, with a bugle-horn badge.

The figures illustrated show the classic 'rifle' uniform and the 'Albert' shako. It is interesting to note that contemporary sources (for example the Ackermann print from which the officer is taken, other prints and Dubois Drahonet's work) show different methods of wearing the girdle, sometimes with the hanging cords looped very low in light infantry style.

This plate is an appropriate place to comment briefly upon the stagnation which built up in the British army after Waterloo, which resulted in a complete lack of organisational and tactical development, so that when faced with a European war (in the Crimea) the unpreparedness of the staff and army as a whole led to the disastrous situation of ancient generals trying to fight a nineteenth-century war with an army and tactics unchanged since 1815. Nowhere was this stagnation more evident than in the army's firearms; hampered by interminable examining boards, the flintlock musket was (largely) retained until the general issue of the 1838 Pattern percussion musket, though some flintlocks were still being used – *on active service* – as late as 1846. The universal issue of rifled firearms was not made until the French Minié design of 1851, though in 1836 the Board of Ordnance sanctioned the issue to rifle regiments of the 'Brunswick' rifle (named from the nationality of its inventor), an appalling weapon completely unfit for use; 'At all distances above four hundred yards the shooting was so wild as to be unrecorded. The Brunswick rifle has shown itself to be much inferior in point of range to any other arm

hitherto noticed. The loading of this rifle is so difficult that it is a wonder how the Rifle regiments have continued to use it so long – the force required to ram down the ball being so great as to render any man's hand unsteady for accurate shooting' (Report of Select Committee on Small Arms, 1852).

Only after the disasters of the Crimean War did British military thinking get apace of other major European powers, though even then it was to some extent due to the efforts and propaganda of those outside the hidebound world of military theory, like Florence Nightingale.

29. Britain:
a) Officer, Light Company, 72nd Highlanders, 1840.
b) Officer, Battalion Company, 78th Ross-shire Buffs, 1834.

While conforming to many infantry regulations, the romantic idea of 'traditional' Highland dress (in fact largely a nineteenth-century invention) resulted in Highland regiments adopting the distinctive uniform which is now so familiar. The bonnet, in imitation of the non-existent 'traditional' head-dress, became progressively more laden with ostrich feathers. Though the kilt and decorative plaid continued in use, when Highland dress was restored to the 71st and 72nd Regiments in 1823 they were given truibhs (trews) of regimental tartan, the 71st (Highland Light Infantry) keeping the dice-banded shako and coupling their light infantry uniform with the new Highland costume, producing a most attractive ensemble.

Though infantry regulations governed the style of jacket, the kilts, plaids and bonnets maintained the Highlanders' individuality, even when officers were ordered to wear white trousers in certain orders of dress. The undress headgear for officers was a small cocked cap with feather until 1829, when a standard bonnet with band of regimental tartan was authorised. Bonnet-plumes were white for all regiments (green for light companies in some cases) though the 42nd's traditional red plumes were officially confirmed. Thistle badges were worn on epaulette-straps and turnbacks by some regiments. Small, purely decorative plaids were worn on occasion, attached to the rear of the shoulder, though the larger version is shown on the 72nd Highlander illustrated; being a light company officer, he also wears wings, bugle-horn badges on the turnbacks, and other details indicative of light troops. Cockade-badges were different for all regiments; that of the 78th illustrated was in the shape of an elephant with a scroll below, while that of the 72nd was a crowned Garter with '72' in the centre. The sporran (only worn with the kilt) was now simply an ornament, different patterns being used by various regiments. In common with all regular officers, gold lace was universally adopted by the Highland corps, though the 92nd retained the traditional black line interwoven in the lace. In 1834 officers' forage caps were altered again, to have a tartan band with an embroidered thistle badge with regimental number below, or regimental badges for those regiments which possessed them.

30. Prussia:
 a) N.C.O.,
  1st Guard Landwehr Regt,
  Service Dress, 1837.
 b) N.C.O.,
  2nd Foot Guards,
  Full Dress, 1830.

While the Russian army copied the Prussian shako after the end of the Napoleonic Wars, the Prussian army was copying Russian patterns! The 2nd Foot Guards uniform illustrated (from a Lieder drawing) included typical Russian items such as the enormous plume, tightly-cut coatee and one-piece gaiter-trousers. Some features (such as the 'Garde-litzen' lace worn by Guard units) were common to both Russian and Prussian armies. In 1824 metal-fronted grenadier caps were issued to the 1st Foot Guards to be worn in full dress (with white overalls), reputedly being the gift of Czar Alexander I, who had presented black cuirasses to the Prussian Garde du Corps, these being worn for parade from 1814.

The Prussian infantry shako (though varying slightly over the years) was bell-topped and worn with the familiar oilskin cover in service dress as before. In 1816 fusiliers of the first thirteen regiments were allowed to wear shako-plates of the Royal cypher instead of their previous lace rosette. The coatee remained dark blue for infantry (laced for Guard units) and green for Jägers, though after 1815 individual facing colours were abolished, collars and cuffs being universally red, with cuff-flaps and shoulder-straps (the latter bearing the regimental number) alternatively red and white by corps. By 1836 grey trousers with red piping were in general use, often worn with brown marching gaiters. In 1817 the Land-wehr (militia) was assimilated into the line, but distinguished from the regulars by blue collar-piping and the traditional white metal cross on the shako.

The 2nd Foot Guards were formed in 1813 from a training battalion, and did not adopt the Guard 'litzen' on the cuffs until 1834. The other figure (taken from a picture by L. Elsholtz) shows the uniform of the Guard Landwehr Regiment, and also the standard service dress of the Prussian infantry, including the shako-cover and shoulder-roll always associated with the Prussian army, this latter being not only a convenient way of carrying the greatcoat, but acting as a protection against sabre-cuts as well.

31. Belgium:
  a) Trumpeter,
     1st Chasseurs à Cheval,
     1833.
  b) Officer,
     Guides de la Meuse
     (Gids van de Maas),
     1831.

Belgian cavalry uniforms, even those of the hastily-raised volunteers of 1830–31, always resembled those of the French army, a feature most marked in the two light cavalry uniforms illustrated.

The Guides de la Meuse wore lancer costume with a plume in the national colours of black, yellow and red. Their shabraques were dark blue, pointed-ended, with a red lace border and a black sheepskin saddle-cover edged with red 'wolf teeth'. Other lancer units wore similar patterns – the 1st Lancers in 1832, for example, wore dark blue uniforms with crimson collar, lapels and piping, and crimson trousers with double silver stripe (for officers), the crimson facing-colour being repeated on the czapka-tops.

The Chasseurs à Cheval wore a French-style green uniform with regimental distinctions; the 2nd Regiment in 1833 for example wore tall, red cloth shakos with white lace and drooping plumes, red collar, turn-backs and piping, and red trouser-stripes, their trumpeters having a colourful uniform of the pattern shown in the figure of the 1st Regiment illustrated, but with red jacket laced white and ordinary green trousers. Shabraques were of the pattern described above, of dark green with an edging of the facing colour. Although the 1st Regiment wore yellow facings, their trumpeters had the light blue costume illustrated. The usual head-dress was a tall shako, which in 1838 was made of green cloth and had a drooping green plume, and bore the national cockade on the front. The regimental number was carried in metal on the flap of the black leather pouch.

Lancer trumpeters also wore elab-orate uniforms; those of the 1st Regiment in 1835, for example, had white jackets with crimson lapels, collar and piping, dark blue trousers with double crimson stripe, red epaulettes and czapkas with crimson tops, red cords and drooping white plumes.

The Guides of the newly-formed Belgian army wore another typically-French uniform; for officers, a large black fur busby with silver cords, white plume and red bag, short green jacket with red lapels, turnbacks and piping, with silver epaulettes, silver-laced pouch-belt, voluminous red trousers with double silver stripes, and dark green shabraques edged red, bearing a silver cypher in the rear corners, with black sheepskin saddle-covers with red cloth edging. The uniforms of other branches of the army were also closely-based upon current French styles, while that of the Gendarmerie was a near copy of the dress worn by the Elite Gendarmes of Napoleon's Imperial Guard.

32. Russia:
a) Officer,
   Tartars of the Guard, 1835.
b) Trooper,
   Guard Hussar Squadron, Service Dress, 1835.

After the Napoleonic Wars the Russian army (except the troops in the Caucasus) became a mechanical machine which could drill to the utmost perfection but which, had it been severely tried, would have suffered from lack of field training. The drill itself – tuned to perfection by endless practice – produced its folk-heroes, however, like Sergeant Kozhemiakin of the Semenovski Guard Regiment, who when performing the foot-drill, 'his legs were raised completely parallel to the ground and the toe of his boot formed one straight line with his whole leg'; not only was this sergeant a virtual contortionist, but he could do the whole thing with a full glass of water balanced on his head – and not spill a drop!

Plates 32–34 (taken from contemporary prints), while illustrating the uniform of various Guard regiments, also show the general pattern of Russian uniforms, excepting that the coloured lapels and 'litzen' were reserved for Guard units alone.

The massive reviews which provided Nicholas I with an interest in life were golden opportunities to display the elaborate, often exotic, costume worn by the Russian army. The reviews, incidentally, were often costly – during one at Vosnesensk, for example, no less than 700 horses died of exhaustion.

The Tartars of the Guard wore one of the most exotic uniforms of all, being an attempted 'romanticisation' of what was originally a 'national costume'. The bulbous cap, very long-sleeved jacket with imitation cartridge-tubes on the breast and the 'baggy' trousers were all taken from this earlier style. The other figure in this plate illustrates the uniform of the Guard Hussar Squadron, made a little less ornate than normal by the oilskin shako-cover worn on service and by the pelisse being worn as a jacket, to conceal the dolman. Of especial note was the extremely short-barrelled carbine worn on the shoulder-belt. Russian hussar regiments were traditionally the most colourful of the Russian army, which fact can be seen from the following chart of brief uniform-details of line hussar regiments in 1840.

Regt	Dolman	Pelisse	Lace	Shako & Sabretache	Shab-raque
1. Sumsk	Grey	Grey	White	Red	Grey
2. Klastiz	Dark blue	Dark blue	White	Light blue	Dark blue
3. Elisabethgrad	Grey	Grey	Orange-yellow	Grey	Grey
4. Luben	Dark blue	Dark blue	White	Yellow	Dark blue
5. Wittgenstein	Dark blue	Dark blue	Orange-yellow	Yellow	Dark blue
6. Prince of Oranien	Light blue	Red	White	Light blue	Light blue
7. Pavlograd	Green	Light blue	Orange-yellow	Light blue	Green
8. Archduke Ferdinand	Red	Dark blue	White	Red	Dark blue
9. Achtirsk	Brown	Brown	Orange-yellow	Yellow	Brown
10. Alexandrien	Dark blue	Dark blue	White	Red	Dark blue
11. Kiev	Green	Green	Orange-yellow	Red	Green
12. Ingermanland	Light blue	Light blue	Orange-yellow	Light blue	Light blue
13. Michael Pavlovich	Light blue	Light blue	White	Light blue	Light blue
14. King of Württemburg	Green	Green	White	Light blue	Green

33. Russia:
a) Officer, Chevaliers Guards, Full Dress, 1835.
b) Drum-Major, Palace Guard, 1835.

The Chevaliers Guards, raised by Peter the Great, wore a uniform styled like that of the Russian cuirassiers, with the enormous, crested helmet. Like the heavy bodyguard cavalry of numerous German states (Plate 10), they wore the traditional white uniform. The officer illustrated is in full dress, without the gilt cuirass with red 'cuffs' worn on most occasions. Blue-grey trousers with red piping were also worn. Musicians had a particularly magnificent version of this dress, including scarlet helmet-crest, silver edging to the collar, gold epaulettes worn over gold-laced wings, and with the breast and sleeves of the coatee covered with gold lace. Even the kettledrummer's white gauntlets had gold lace fringes!

Other Guard units, the Life Guard Cuirassiers and the Horse Guards, wore similar uniforms, the former with light blue facings and black-enamelled cuirasses bearing gilt eagle-plates on the front, and the latter with red facings and gilt cuirasses. Officers of all used black sword-knots with silver tassels; note also the heavy-tasselled silver sash worn by the officer illustrated.

The shako being examined by the Chevalier Guard is that of a musician of the Life Guard Grenadiers, with the large 'eagle' plate which Guard units continued to use even though the Line pattern was changed periodically. Different ranks wore different-coloured versions of the enormous plume: the print from which this head-dress is taken, for example, shows the drum-major with a white-tipped red plume, and an N.C.O. with a white-tipped black one. An unusual feature peculiar to the Russian army was the use of a metal scroll inscribed FOR DISTINGUISHED SERVICE, worn above the shako-plate by deserving recipients.

The Palace Grenadiers were raised in 1827, composed of 250 hand-picked veterans to act as a personal bodyguard to the Czar following the Decembrist plot. Their uniform was a deliberate imitation of that worn by Napoleon's Guard Grenadiers, and was among the most magnificent in an army remarkable for the magnificence of its dress (though some orders of dress comprised a much plainer costume than the full dress illustrated). It is interesting to note that the Prussian 'Schloss-garde-kom-panie' or Royal bodyguard was copied directly from the Czar's Palace Grenadiers. The drum-major shown illustrates how Russian musicians' uniforms were often literally covered with gold lace or braid. A common practice throughout Europe was to appoint the most distinguished-look-ing man in the regiment to act as drum-major, and the Russian army was no exception. It was reported that one Ivan Stepanovich Lushkin (1811–44), drum-major of the Preobraz-henski Guards, measured no less than 3 arshin 9¼ vershok (8 feet 3¾ inches). His left femur and tibia are preserved in the Museum of the Academy of Sciences in Leningrad, but indicate a height of a mere 7 feet 10¼ inches!

34. Russia:
a) Trooper,
   Guard Lancer Regiment,
   Service Dress, 1835.
b) N.C.O.,
   Grenadier Regiment
   Pavlovski,
   Service Dress, 1835.

This plate shows how the brass-fronted grenadier cap (see Plate 4) was worn with a waterproof cover in service dress, with the coatee-lapels buttoned over to conceal the facing colour. Nicholas I introduced trousers for the army (white for summer and green for winter), and made the jackets of all but the Guard units single-breasted.

The Guard Lancer Squadron nor-mally wore czapkas with red tops, gilt eagle plates and woollen ball-tufts, had the lapels fastened back to show the red facing-colour, and wore blue trousers with double red stripe, but in service dress (as illus-trated here) the czapka-cover, over-alls and buttoned-over lapels were used. Officers had gold lace and epaulettes; shabraques were rounded-ended, dark blue, with red and yellow lace edging and bearing the Imperial cypher in red (gold for officers) in the rear corners.

Other corps of the Russian army (Dragoons and Artillery) retained their dark green uniforms and the lancers their dark blue; the Cossacks, though still dressed in their individual manner with fur cap, had uniforms of a more regulation cut than before; like the British Highlanders and the Russian Guard Tartars (Plates 29 and 32), their uniform was a manu-factured travesty of original national dress. Dragoons and Artillery wore the infantry pattern shako, but the Marines had a tapering version. In 1844 (a year later than the Prussians although the design was originally Russian), the spike-topped leather helmet was introduced for all regiments previously wearing shakos, the 'spike' being in the form of a bursting grenade; cuirassiers adopted this head-dress in 1845 as a temporary measure before receiving a custom-made metal version in 1846.

Fortunately for that country, not all Russian units were drill-automatons; the Army of the Caucasus, constantly on active service, maintained the army's contact with reality. From about 1829 they began to evolve their own style of dress, with appearance disregarded and only efficiency and comfort considered. The élite Nijergorodski Dragoons (raised 1834), for example, wore a tall fur shako, loose blouses and 'baggy' trousers in original cossack style, and carried shashquas (cossack sabres) worn from a shoulder-belt. Like the dress evolved by the British in India and the French in Algeria, their uniform was not attractive but was superb for campaigning.

An interesting story is attached to the adoption of the spiked helmet. In 1840 a peasant girl discovered an ancient helmet near Lipeltz, which was identified as that belonging to Jaroslav Vsevolodovitch, Prince of Muscovy, who fought at the Battle of Lipeltz in 1216. The Czar was most impressed by this discovery, and decided that a helmet should replace the shako as the army's principal headgear. The first pattern of helmet was issued to the Corps of Pages, an aristocratic officer-school, which that unit retained until 1917.

35. Denmark:
a) Overjäger (N.C.O.), Fyenske Infanterie, 1837.
b) Officer, Livgarde til Hest (Lifeguard), 1837.

Both uniforms illustrated in this plate are taken from Bruun's *Danske Uniformer* (1837), and show the old-style Danish uniform. The Livgarde til Hest, like many European body-guard cavalry units, wore the crested helmet, cuirass and light-coloured uniform. The traditional infantry red uniform was also retained and became as ornate as those of other European states. An interesting feature of this uniform is the powder-flask hung from the belt, an item used by the 'rifle' units of several nations; the N.C.O. illustrated also wears the green distinctions and badges traditionally associated with light infantry and rifle corps.

The Danish army was reorganised and modernised in 1842. A bell-topped infantry shako was retained but of much plainer form, and the red coatee was also simplified. Light blue trousers were the usual wear, the white ones (and white shako-cords) being reserved for full dress. Infantry titles were replaced by battalion numbers.

Thigh-length tunics were introduced for Jägers and engineers in 1842, though the ordinary infantry had the coatee. The Jäger units had red and black facings and piping to their dark green tunics, and infantry_ style shakos with green ball-tufts, but the undress cap (with a flat cloth top and leather peak, of green with red piping) was frequently worn instead. Musicians of all arms wore laced wings of the same colour as the collar (Jägers had red wings). Tunics of this pattern, of dark blue with red piping and collar-patches, replaced the red infantry uniform in 1848, dragoons (previously wearing red with yellow trimming) adopting the same style with crimson distinctions. Engineers had worn all-blue tunics from 1842, and these (with crimson trimming) were adopted by artillery units in 1848. It had been intended to issue a black leather, spiked helmet of Prussian pattern with the tunic, but the outbreak of the 1st Schleswig War in 1848 prevented its emergence, the 1848 field cap (a light blue képi) being common wear in place of the shako. The 2nd Jägers, in fact, conveniently 'lost' their shakos so that they could take the field in the more serviceable and comfortable cloth cap! Even at this time, the infantry wore the old light blue trousers, but the war resulted in the more rapid issue of the tunic than had been intended, thereby hastening the modernisation of Danish uniform. Equipment was generally of the old style (black leather with white haversacks, skin pouches with coloured cloth straps – red being common), the new Prussian-style equipment not coming into use until 1850. Jägers and light infantry wore dark grey trousers from 1849.

It should be noted that officers of the Livgarde wore sashes of mixed red and gold, of which only the hanging tails were visible at the rear of the left-hand side of the body, ending in long, heavy tassels. The turnbacks were of the same colour as the body of the coat, edged with red lace and bearing a silver crown device. The black leather sabretache bore a white metal F IV R cypher, with a crown above.

36. Papal States:
Trumpeter,
Artillery of the Foreign
(Swiss) Brigade, 1834.
Switzerland:
Officer,
Artillery,
Canton Zurich, 1837.

Both corps illustrated in this plate wore French-style uniforms, both were artillery, and both were composed of Swiss – but they belonged to different armies.

Following the 1831 revolt in the Papal States, when even the Carabinieri had become involved, it was decided to follow the Neapolitan example and recruit a brigade of Swiss mercenaries who would be less likely to become involved in revolutionary movements than would native Italians. Two regiments of Swiss infantry were formed into the 'Foreign Brigade', and in October 1833 Captain de Lentulus organised a battery of artillery, also Swiss, with a strength of 4 officers and 142 men. Its only active service occurred in 1848, when it participated in the action against the Austrian army at Vincenza. When the Roman Republic was declared the Swiss battery was disbanded and, unlike the infantry, never revived.

The artillery battery wore tall, tapering French-style shakos of black felt with gold lace trimming (red lace for the rank and file), with a brass badge of grenade over crossed cannons, the Papal cockade (white with yellow centre) and a drooping red horsehair plume on the front. Their double-breasted jackets were dark blue with red cuffs, collar-patches, piping and turnbacks, and dark blue trousers with double red stripe and black leather reinforcements. Red epaulettes (gold for officers) were worn on the jacket and the dark blue greatcoat. The trumpeter illustrated (taken from *Li Customi Militari Pontifici* [1834]) shows the French style of clothing musicians in not only different colours but entirely different styles from the remainder of the corps. The busby, lace loops on the breast and voluminous trousers were all typical of French hussar-style costume.

It was not until 1852 that a universal uniform was adopted in Switzerland; prior to that date, the forces of each canton maintained individual distinctions. The officer of the Zurich Artillery illustrated (taken from a print by J. K. Sperli) shows another French-style uniform, not unlike that of the Papal battery. The tapering shako bore the common crossed-cannons badge, and the light blue and white Zurich cockade had an unusual gilt-scaled strap attaching it to the shako. The pouch-badge bore the crossed-cannons device also, with an exploding grenade badge in addition; turnback-badges were gold grenades for officers and red for other ranks; who wore red epaulettes

instead of the officers' gold. Other ranks were armed with brass-hilted short sabres; leather equipment was white, with calfskin packs, usually worn with a rolled greatcoat carried in a red-and-white striped cover on top of the pack. Other ranks had red piping on the trousers, drivers having black leather reinforcing as well.

37. France:
a) Trooper, 2nd Lancers, 1840.
b) Private, Artillery Train, Garde Royale, 1824.

This plate illustrates two branches of the French army not previously mentioned. The uniform of the Artillery Train of the Royal Guard illustrated is strongly reminiscent (in colouring) of its equivalent in Napoleon's army. The helmet, bearing the Royal arms on the front, was a development of the style adopted immediately after Waterloo, being similar to the 1792 fur-crested helmet originally copied from the British 'Tarleton'.

Whereas most armies after 1815 included Lancer units, this famous branch of the French army was almost totally disbanded, only the Lancers of the Royal Guard maintaining the tradition; they wore dark green uniforms with crimson facings and czapkas. In 1830 this regiment was replaced by Louis Philippe's Lanciers d'Orléans, wearing green faced yellow with red trousers and czapka, and five more regiments were raised in 1831, the Lanciers d'Orléans becoming the 6th in the line. In 1837 the eight regiments (two more had been added in 1836) adopted the uniform shown in this plate, the first four having yellow facings and the remainder red; the red plume was introduced in 1839. An interesting feature was the 'tricolor' lance-pennon.

The other light cavalry arm, the Hussars, though completely reorganised after 1815, continued to wear their splendid costume. The usual hussar dress with tall shako was worn by all regiments except the Guard Hussars, who had blue uniforms with 'amaranth' facings and wore busbies. In 1816 the line hussar regiments were uniformed as shown in the first chart.

shako and trousers, and the 9th a sombre, black costume. To provide one detailed description of hussar uniform at this period, the following details of the 1st Regiment are taken from a contemporary print: shako shaped like those in Plate 36, of red cloth with black leather fittings; cockade secured by a loop of white lace, with red cords looped on to the breast and a drooping, black horsehair plume; sky-blue dolman with red cuffs, sky-blue collar edged red, with red braid and white metal buttons; sky-blue pelisse with black fur, red

Regiment	Dolman & Pelisse	Trousers
1. du Jura	Sky blue	Scarlet
2. de la Meurthe	Brown	Sky blue
3. de la Moselle	Grey	Crimson
4. du Nord	Dark green	Scarlet
5. du Bas-Rhin	Royal blue	Scarlet
6. du Haut-Rhin	Dark Grey	Sky blue

The uniform pattern changed gradually as it did for the remainder of the French army, the shako gradually becoming smaller and more tapered. The basic colour-schemes in use in 1834 are shown in the second chart.

In 1840 three more regiments were raised, the 7th wearing a uniform like Napoleon's Guides, the 8th a white dolman and pelisse with sky-blue

braid and white metal buttons; red trousers with black leather reinforcing. White leather pouch- and carbine-belts, with sabre suspended from a waist-belt; brass three-bar hilt, steel scabbard and white sword-knot; black sabretache with shield-shaped brass plate.

It is interesting to note that as late as 1816 some members of the 5th Hussars were still wearing queues

Regiment	Dolman & Pelisse	Trousers & Shako
1.	Sky blue	Madder Red
2.	Brown	Madder Red
3.	Silver-Grey	Madder Red
4.	Madder Red	Sky blue
5.	Dark blue	Madder Red
6.	Green	Madder Red

(pigtails) and side-tresses; when these archaic features were ordered to be removed in that year, about fifty men deserted in disgust!

38. France:
a) Grenadier,
   Légion d'Etranger,
   Service Dress (Spain),
   1837.
b) Officer,
   Light Infantry, 1830

The colour-bearer (taken from a Raffet print) shows the 1822 pattern infantry dress, with the red trousers adopted in 1829 by the French army, allegedly to give work to the dye industry! Probably the reason for their adoption was political; in the last months of the Bourbon régime the basic colouring of the uniform was changed from the Royalist blue and white to the red, white and blue traditionally associated with liberalism and independence; but if the change were politically-inspired, it didn't prevent the 1830 revolution! Note the red, white and blue plume (reserved for certain categories of officers and N.C.O.s), and the Gallic cock surmounting the colour-pole, a universal military symbol adopted in 1830.

The Foreign Legion – perhaps the most famous (and at times infamous) corps in the world – was instituted as the 'Légion d'Etranger' in 1831, a revival of the ancient French practice of employing foreign mercenaries. Raised for service in Algeria, the recruits came from every nation in Europe. Basically organised into three battalions of Germans, and one of each of Spaniards, Italians, Poles and Dutch/Belgians, the Legion included smaller numbers of men from many other nations. Their discipline – throughout history the most savage of any army – was necessary as the vast majority of recruits were deserters from other armies, radicals on the run, adventurers or just plain criminals.

When the first batch of recruits landed at Algiers, an eye-witness compared them, as they marched along singing 'La Parisienne', to a circus; aged between 16 and 60, they wore whatever outdated clothing could be scraped together, uniforms of the National Guard, the Imperial Guard, Royal Guard, infantry, cavalry etc.

From this unlikely body grew perhaps the best – and certainly the toughest – fighting force in history. The legend of the Legion – it might almost be called charisma – was sown as early as May 1832, when a Legion patrol comprising only one officer and 26 légionnaires, was caught in the open by a huge body of Arab horsemen. They stood their ground, and when their bodies were later discovered no less than seventy dead Arabs lay around them.

Perhaps the mystique surrounding the Legion was caused partly by its multi-national composition, where every man owed his allegiance not to a country or king, but to 'La Légion', always 'La Légion'. Its mixed composition had other advantages – the town of Sidi-Bel-Abbes was built by the Legion unaided, as its ranks included professional carpenters, stone-masons and draughtsmen – one company alone included five qualified architects. An interesting example of this cosmopolitan aspect is found in the words of Captain (later Marshal) Saint-Arnaud as he led his company through the breach at Constantine (1837): 'Avanti! Schnell! Good luck! La Légion!'

With the experience of the Algerian campaign behind them, the Foreign Legion were regarded as the ideal troops to send as the French contingent to the Carlist War – and they were expendable. In August 1835 three battalions were *sold* to Spain, and began fighting a brutal, atrocity-ridden war in which they distinguished themselves in the manner which was to become their hallmark. Used as an expendable assault-force trained to die, the 9,000 légionnaires who served in Spain lost 3,600 killed in battle and 4,000 'missing' – genuinely missing, deserted to the enemy or fled over the Pyrenees. Those who were left were decimated by disease and malnutrition. The climax came at the Battle of Barbastro (1838), where the Legion came face to face with the 'foreign legion' of Don Carlos. When Colonel Conrad of the Legion was killed, his men fought with maniacal fury, slaughtering the Carlist 'legion' until only 160 were left alive out of 875. But the French Legion had suffered so badly that they were all but destroyed; when in January 1839 the Legion shuffled out of the war across the Pyrenees, the 9,000 had been reduced to 63 officers and only 159 other ranks.

The Legion wore the standard infantry uniform, with modifications learnt in Algeria – fastening the coat-tails back and tucking the trousers into the gaiters or socks, for example. One item not carried from Algeria where it was extensively worn was the 'schech', a muslin face-wrap used to protect the face from sandstorms. Virtually abandoned in Spain, however, their clothing became progressively more patched, then ragged, then fell to pieces. Boots were replaced by Spanish sandals where avilable, or bundles of rags, and the figure illustrated wears a captured Carlist beret in place of the regulation shako. Even the officers came to resemble bandits instead of soldiers: Major Jean-Louis Lebeau, Colonel Conrad's predecessor and a veteran of the retreat from Moscow and Waterloo, was the very opposite of his name; wearing an old tramp's hat, a ragged coat without epaulettes, trousers which hardly reached his knees, a pair of broken boots with long spurs, and carrying a Turkish scimitar on a piece of string round his neck, Major Lebeau trudged around with eyes lowered as if ashamed to be seen resembling a walking rag-bag!

39. Spain:
  a) Trooper,
     Navarrese Cavalry, 1838.
  b) Officer,
     Arlaban Hussars,
     1838.
  c) Trooper,
     Guipuzcoan Cavalry, 1838.

The Carlist forces were characterised by a uniquely-Spanish head-dress, the coloured, frequently-tasselled beret. Due mainly to chronic shortages of equipment, uniforms were generally simple, though some units did possess more exotic costumes, at least for a time. Cavalry squadrons, usually numbering about 100 men, were not organised in permanent regimental bodies, each squadron retaining its independent identity and uniform. The number of squadrons varied considerably: both the Carlist Army of the North and Army of the Centre had only two squadrons each in 1834, but by 1836 the North had fifteen and by 1839 the Centre fourteen; those of the Centre were later organised on a more 'regimental' basis of three or four squadrons each, one regiment (the Tortosa) even having a band. Because of the shortage of firearms, the lance was the most common weapon.

The sheepskin horse-furniture was almost universal, often edged with coloured cloth (white for the Army of the Centre). Equipment was generally of white leather for the Centre and black for the North. The Navarrese Cavalry (illustrated) also possessed white cloaks (red for trumpeters, who on at least one occasion wore costume 'borrowed' from a troop of itinerant actors!) Among other Northern squadrons, the Castillian and Biscayan wore uniforms like the Navarrese; the Alava Cavalry wore light blue jackets with red collars and cuffs, red beret, and dark red or grey trousers; the Aragonese had red berets and dark red trousers and probably brown jackets; the Merino Cavalry had yellow jackets, with beret and trousers like the Alava, and red-and-black lance-pennons. In addition to the Arlaban Hussars (illustrated), the Northern Army included two troops of Guard Cavalry who didn't carry lances, the 24-strong 'Guardia de Honor' who had blue uniforms with red collar, cuffs and trouser-stripe,

and red berets with blue tassels, and the 'Standard Escort', wearing a similar uniform but with silver beret-tassels.

The Centre cavalry as a rule was much worse equipped and uniformed, but still had individual dress wherever possible. The élite Tortosa Lancers (including a squadron of 'Tiradores' armed with carbines) had white berets with red and yellow tassel, sky-blue jackets with red wings and turnbacks, and grey trousers with yellow stripes; the Tiradores had dark blue berets, yellow dolmans with green collars and cuffs and mixed green-and-red braid, and light blue trousers. The two regiments of Aragonese Lancers of the Centre had red berets with white tassels and green jackets, while the Valencia Lancers had red berets and dark blue jackets with red turnbacks. The Ontorio Hussars wore a uniform like that of the Arlaban, with red or red-and-green braid and probably black lance-pennons with white skull and crossed bones device. General Cabrera's veteran bodyguard, the Orderlies of the General, wore green berets with red tassels, red dolmans with black fur collars and cuffs and green braid, and blue trousers with red stripes; they were merged with the Tortosa Lancers in 1839.

Other Centre cavalry were dressed in everything from rags to civilian dress, often having little uniformity. Two squadrons from La Mancha – one of Lancers and one of Tiradores – wore tall black hats, dark blue jackets and breeches, brown leggings and red sashes, virtually a civilian costume; only the officers had white berets with gold or silver tassels. They were armed with a variety of weapons, including blunderbusses. The Lancers of El Cid were so ill-equipped that they had pack-saddle and ropes instead of saddles and bridles, and their 'lances' were poles with a nail at the top!

CAMPAIGNS IN SOUTH AMERICA, 1815–50

Military operations in South America were dominated by the liberal independence movement inspired by the French Revolution and the French invasions of Spain and Portugal; the resident Spanish and native population of South America rose to overthrow the European domination of the continent and turn the colonies into self-governing, independent states. From the beginning of the century various revolts had attempted to shake off the Spanish yoke, but only in Argentina (independent in all but name since 1810) and Paraguay had any real success been achieved. Independence was finally assured by the efforts of two remarkable men – Simon Bolivar and José de San Martin, both of whom led 'liberation armies' which included foreign mercenaries, principally from Britain, Germany and North America.

Having been defeated in command of the armies of two would-be independent states, Venezuela and Colombia, Bolivar in 1815 was in exile in the West Indies. In 1816 he returned to Venezuela at the head of a new revolutionary movement, winning a victory near Barcelona (16 February), but was defeated heavily at La Puerta in March 1818. Undismayed, Bolivar marched his 2,500 ill-equipped men across the Andes and into Colombia; placing his force between the Spanish army in garrison there and the capital, Bogota, Bolivar inflicted a decisive defeat at the Battle of Boyaca (7 August 1819), thanks largely to the performance of his veteran 'British Legion'. Appointed President of the now-independent Colombia, Bolivar continued his war against the Spanish garrison armies with little success, with a six months' armistice in 1820–21. A victory at Carabobo (25 June 1821) – again largely due to the determination of the British Legion – resulted in the capture of Caracas, and in 1822 Bolivar moved on into Quito Province. Despite Bolivar's check at Bombino (7 April 1822), his general Sucre won a victory at Pichincha (24 May 1822) which captured Quito itself.

Meanwhile, San Martin had been equally active. A Peninsular War veteran, he returned to Buenos Aires in 1810 and began to train a 'liberation' Army of the Andes, part Argentinian and part Chilean. When Argentina officially declared her independence in 1816, San Martin began to move. Marching over the Andes with 3,700 men and 21 guns – a monumental feat – San Martin and his Irish–Chilean subordinate, Bernardo O'Higgins, won a crushing victory for negligible loss at Chacabuco (12–13 February 1817) and Chilean independence became fact. A Spanish force marched from Peru to recapture the lost colony; San Martin was defeated at Cancha-Rayada (16 March 1818), but re-grouped and three weeks later flung the Spaniards back into Peru by a victory on the River Maipu. A liberation of Peru was impossible, however, while the Spaniards controlled the sea. At this opportune moment, an ex-Royal Navy officer, Lord Thomas Cochrane, arrived to join San Martin and was put in command of the Chilean 'navy'. Described as insane and violent by his previous British superiors, Cochrane was an audacious leader whose contributions were vital. Having previously turned down an offer to command the Spanish navy, he sailed his flagship the 'O'Higgins' (a captured Spanish frigate) into Valdiva harbour in June 1820, landed a shore party and captured the defences. With the last Spanish foothold in Chile broken, San Martin invaded Peru.

An amphibious landing on the Peruvian coast, another raid by Cochrane, and Peru fell. San Martin then began to advance towards Bolivar's army, coming from the north, to link up and complete their joint work of liberation. Meeting at Guayaquil in July 1822, Bolivar assumed command of the combined armies. San Martin, a simple patriot of high military skill, turned over all command to the politically-ambitious Bolivar and retired from the scene. Spanish rule in South America was finally ended by the Battle of Junin (6 August 1824) – a cavalry action with reputedly not a shot fired by either side – and the Battle of Ayacucho (9 December 1824), when the Spanish suffered their most crushing defeat of all, including fourteen generals captured.

Brazil, the sole Portuguese colony in the continent, declared her independence in September 1822, with Don Pedro crowned as Emperor. Thomas Cochrane, now in command of the Brazilian navy, virtually decided the issue single-handed; the Portuguese, in an attempt to suppress the rebellion, put their entire force aboard transports and headed for Maranhao; Cochrane, in faster-moving frigates, got there ahead of them and captured the port, leaving the Portuguese only one alternative – to sail home to Portugal! Brazilian independence was recognised in 1825.

Mexico suffered from a series of bitter rebellions and resulting atrocity, until the Spanish commander, General Iturbide, revolted against his masters and crowned himself Emperor Agustin I (21 July 1822). In less than a year he too had been toppled from his throne by a revolution, and a republic was established. In Central America,

Spanish control gradually crumbled, and the area passed into Mexican hands after 1821. After Iturbide's fall, however, a state calling itself the United Province of Central America asserted its independence.

Once South America had been liberated, the new nation-states began to fight each other as revolution, revolt and massacre followed the appointment of every new dictator. In 1825–28 a combined Argentinian–Uruguayan force wrested the area now known as Uruguay from Brazilian control. Peru, in a burst of expansionist fever, captured Bolivia (1827) and invaded Ecuador. Bolivar's old lieutenant, Sucre, now President of Bolivia, defeated the Peruvians at Tarqui (1829) and ended the invasion. In 1829 Spain launched an abortive expedition to reconquer Mexico, but was driven off. In 1835 a confederation of Peru and Bolivia was formed; Chile opposed the move, declared war, and smashed the alliance at Yungay (1839). In 1838–39 a French expeditionary force invaded Mexico to protect the rights of French citizens there. 1841 saw Peru invade their erstwhile ally, Bolivia, only to be repelled at the Battle of Ingavi. Santo Domingo (the eastern portion of Haiti) revolted against the Haitian government in 1844 and won their independence. Between 1843 and 1852 a confused and confusing war was waged, beginning with an Argentinian attempt to take advantage of a revolt in Uruguay and annex that country. After a revolt in Argentina, intervention by Brazil, France and Britain, the matter was ended when the Argentinian dictator Juan de Rosas was beaten at Caseros (1852) by a combined force of Uruguayans, Brazilians – and other Argentinians!

It is interesting to note, in passing, that the 'mercenary' element in the South American wars of liberation was principally British. While Cochrane and a few others are well-known, the contributions of many more should not be forgotten. San Martin raised a whole regiment, the Cazadores Ingleses, from the British population of Buenos Aires, while the bulk of virtually all South American navies were commanded by British officers. In the Argentine–Brazilian war of 1825–28, for example, the naval campaign was largely waged by Englishmen on both sides, perhaps accounting for its ferocity; not only were the officers British, but the Brazilian navy alone contained no less than 1,200 British seamen, mostly deserters from merchantmen at Brazilian ports.

Two other British commanders played outstanding roles in South American warfare; William Miller, a Peninsular veteran, who achieved great fame as leader of a marine corps operating from Cochrane's fleet, was an indefatigable soldier and must have been the most shot-holed man in the continent. In campaigning in Chile and Peru he received musket-balls in both arms, chest and back, a crippled hand, a crushed foot, a thigh broken by grapeshot and a badly-scarred face caused by the explosion of a Congreve rocket. It was the charge of his hussars at Ayacucho which captured the Spanish artillery and finally decided the battle. William Brown was an Irish sailor-of-fortune who commanded the Argentinian navy in both the wars of liberation and in the Argentinian–Brazilian war. The stories of his dash and enterprise are legendary; it is said that he once attacked a stranded Brazilian ship with cavalry and, on running out of roundshot on another occasion, ordered the guns to be loaded with hard Dutch cheeses rather than break off the engagement!

In the game of political musical chairs which formed Latin American military history of this period, official uniforms were based on European – and in particular Napoleonic – models, frequently having a Franco–Spanish flavour. However, it should be noted that although Plates 40–42 show uniforms of great magnificence, the actual combat dress of the majority of Latin American armies usually consisted of semi-civilian, semi-military, semi-ragbag clothing with whatever weapons could be issued, captured or stolen. Even general officers combined incongrous items of civilian dress with their dress uniforms; a portrait of General William Miller, for example, shows him wearing a regulation low-crowned bicorn hat, single-breasted coatee with heavily-laced collar and cuffs, laced trousers and large-rowelled spurs, but with almost the whole of the coatee and half the trousers covered by a cloth 'poncho', edged all round with braid and with a gold-laced neck-hole.

SOUTH AMERICAN UNIFORMS 1815–50 (Plates 40–42)

40. Andean Liberation Army:
  a) Officer,
  Mounted Chasseurs, 1820.
  b) Trooper,
  Horse Grenadiers, with the Banner of the Army of the Andes, 1817.

These uniforms are a typical combination of the style of Napoleonic France and the traditional over-embellished and at times downright impractical costumes favoured by the Spanish. The Horse Grenadier carrying the Liberation Army banner wears regulation dress, though it should be noted that in 1817 the shako-cords were yellow and the plume green. Lances were carried by other ranks, with white over yellow pennons, later changed to light blue and white squares. The shako-plate bore the national arms over a shield embossed with crossed cannon-barrels and a bursting grenade. The Horse Grenadiers had an élite company wearing tail-less blue jackets with red piping, red pelisses with black fur and braid, and white metal helmets in French dragoon style, with black caterpillar crest, leopardskin turban and brass chinscales; their sword-knots were red.

The Squadron of Mounted Chasseurs was raised from the Horse Grenadiers in February 1817 as the Chasseurs of the Gral, later designated the Mounted Chasseur Squadron. Troopers wore a similar uniform to that depicted, without the lace, epaulettes and sash and with white braid. The bag of the odd, fur-covered shako was unlaced for troopers. The aiguillettes were silver for officers and mixed light blue and white for other ranks. An 'honour badge' was worn above the left cuff, of silver embroidery for officers and red on dark blue for other ranks, bearing a laurel wreath and the words LA PATRIA A LOS VENCEDORES DE MAIPU – ABRIL 5 DE 1818 (The Nation to the victors of Maipu – April 5 1818). A similar uniform is shown in the painting 'La Revista de Rancagua' by J. M. Blanes (National History Museum, Buenos Aires), in which an officer is shown with fringeless epaulettes and a steel-scabbarded sword. The Squadron was disbanded in 1821.

In contrast to the ornate uniform of his troops, San Martin himself favoured a more simple costume, consisting of black bicorn with national cockade, dark blue/black long-tailed coat and breeches with gold epaulettes, laced collar and cuffs, black riding-boots, light blue sashes over the left shoulder and waist, and a 'mameluke'-hilted sabre with red knot worn from a white waistband with rectangular gilt plate.

Features of the two uniforms illustrated, but which cannot be seen in the plate, include the yellow cloth grenade-badge in the rear corner of the Horse Grenadiers' shabraque, the silver sword-knot of the Chasseur officer (that of the Horse Grenadiers was white), and the Chasseur's waist-belt plate, a rectangular gilt plate with cut corners and bearing an embossed hunting-horn. The Banner of the Army of the Andes bore in the central oval a brown mountain-peak on a white background, with two natural-coloured arms holding a brown staff surmounted by a red Phrygian cap, the half of the central oval nearest to the staff being light blue. The central panel was surmounted by a gold rising sun, and had a green laurel-wreath surround. The body of the flag was divided vertically into light blue and white sections.

41. Argentina:
   a) 2nd Sergeant,
      5th Chasseurs,
      Summer Dress, 1826.
   b) Colonel,
      16th Lancers, 1826.
   c) Trooper,
      3rd Cuirassiers, 1826.

These uniforms were worn by the Argentinian army during the 1825–28 war against Brazil; they maintain the characteristic Franco–Spanish style.

An interesting feature of the cuirassier (based on a J. M. Blanes painting, 'Coracero de Lavalle') was the regimental number worn in yellow silk on the left upper arm. The infantry uniform (here shown by the chasseur sergeant) was worn with dark blue trousers and gaiters in winter. Most branches of the army wore similar uniforms – the 7th Cavalry, for example, wore dark blue cloth-covered shakos with brass National Arms plate, dark green plume and black cords, dark blue coatee with red piping on the collar, cuffs, turnbacks and lapels, blue trousers with red stripe and the regimental number worn on the left upper arm.

The 16th Lancers were raised in 1826 under the veteran Colonel José de Olivarria and was regarded as one of the best units in the army; at the Battle of Ituzaingo, for example, they were reported as fighting in formation, 'as though on parade', even capturing an enemy battery. The uniform illustrated is based on a portrait of Colonel Olivarria by A. P. Goulu, and must have been one of the most ornate ever worn in a continent known for ornate uniforms! A painting of Ituzaingo, however, shows a plainer, more serviceable uniform worn by an officer: black shako with yellow upper band and brass plate, dark green single-breasted jacket with red collar, cuffs and pocket-piping, green turnbacks and gold epaulettes, dark green trousers with red stripe, and a plain sabre in a black leather, brass-mounted scabbard. Other ranks wore dark green cloth-covered shakos with white upper band and cords, brass plates and white metal chin-scales, all dark green with white braid

on the collar, breast and cuffs, white epaulettes, and white-edged turnbacks; dark green trousers with double white stripe, white leather equipment and high black riding-boots; red over white lance-pennons. Other ranks' shabraques were dark green, square-cut, with white borders; officers apparently used long-tailed shabraques with red edges, and dark green valises bearing the regimental number in white.

The unit was disbanded in 1829.

42. **Argentina:**
   a) **Private,**
      1st Infantry Bn,
      'Patricios',
      Full Dress, 1842.
   Brazilian Empire:
   b) **Trumpeter,**
      National Guard Hussars,
      Full Dress (Winter
      Uniform), 1840.

The uniform of the Argentinian 1st Infantry – the famous 'Patricios' corps raised in 1806 and possessing a record of outstanding distinction – shows how the original 'Napoleonic' styles of South American uniform gave way to fashions following the current European costume; by the 1860's, for example, the French tunic, baggy trousers and képi had all been adopted by the Argentinian army. The uniform illustrated shows the tapering shako, bearing the light blue and white National cockade and the regimental number on shako-plate and pompom, and repeated on the belt-plate. The red ribbon affixed to the left breast commemorates the red shield worn on the sleeves of the original unit in the 1806–07 British invasion, when they began their remarkable career; the red shield is worn to this day. Besides the blue full dress uniform shown, the regiment had two more – one all-red and the other all-white, worn alternatively by seasons or for different services.

The Brazilian uniform (taken from *Uniformes de la Guardia Nacional* by J. M. de Costa Araujo, 1840) shows a magnificent musician's dress. The coat of arms of the Brazilian Empire is visible on the cap-plate and belt-plate. The uniform of the ordinary National Guard Hussars was very different from that worn by musicians; officers had French-style czapkas with red cloth top edged gold, black skull and peak with gilt edging, gilt 'sunburst' plate bearing the Imperial arms in silver, gilt chin-scales, red and white drooping feather plume and gold cap-lines; red dolman with blue collar and pointed cuffs and a large amount of hussar-style braid ing, blue pelisse with black fur and much gold braid, dark blue trousers with red-edged double gold stripes; crimson corded sash with gold tassels, white waist- and pouch-belts, the former with a gilt plate bearing the Imperial arms; blue shabraque with triple gold lace border and bearing an Imperial crown on the pistol-holsters.

The costume of other South American armies followed similar patterns; both Venezuelan and Chilean troops were primarily dressed in light blue in the 1820's, though one notable exception was Bolivar's Venezuelan Bodyguard corps, whose uniform was styled from that of Napoleon's Imperial Guard Chasseurs à Cheval. This colourful unit wore (in 1820) a white fur busby with red bag and upright white plume rising from gilt ball-socket, scarlet dolman with much yellow–gold braiding in traditional hussar pattern, scarlet breeches with the same braid, including elaborate Austrian knots on the thighs, black Hessian boots with yellow–gold braid and tassels, white pouch-belt and gauntlets, straight-bladed, brass three-bar-hilted sword with red knot and steel scabbard, and barrelled sash of yellow, scarlet and light blue.

For summer-wear on active service, white linen or cotton uniforms were very popular throughout South America, often cut in regulation style, with coloured facings and regulation head-dress, but frequently basically civilian clothing with military accoutrements.

OPERATIONS IN NORTH AMERICA, 1815–46

Between the end of the War of 1812 and the beginning of the U.S.–Mexican War, the United States was not involved in any campaigns against foreign opposition. The only serious military operations were conducted by part-regular and part-volunteer forces against hostiles in the frontier regions. In 1818 General Jackson invaded Spanish Florida to avenge the depredations of the marauding Seminole Indians, returning the territory to Spain at the end of the expedition, but the United States later acquired it (1819). The continued westward expansion brought the Americans into continuous contact with the Indian tribes, naturally resentful of the appropriation of their lands, and constant skirmishing ensued. Most serious was the Black Hawk War of 1832, named after the Sac and Fox chief who led a rising, suppressed by Colonel Zachary Taylor's 400 regulars and 900 militia at the Battle of the Bad Ax (2 August).

The second Seminole War dragged on from 1835 to 1843, a bitter and sanguinary struggle waged among the Florida swamps. In the running guerrilla war led by the chief Osceola, there were two notable actions: in December 1835 a force of 150 regulars was ambushed in Wahoo Swamp, only three men surviving the massacre; and the Battle of Lake Okeechobee exactly two years later when Taylor stormed a Seminole position and broke the back of the rebellion, which nevertheless lasted for four more years. Apart from a minor insurrection in Rhode Island (the Dorr Rebellion) in 1842, the United States was involved in no other serious campaigning until 1846.

There was one other notable (though numerically small) campaign, begun in 1835 when the American settlers in the Mexican-controlled province of Texas revolted against the brutal megalomaniac dictator of Mexico, General Santa Anna. The Mexicans were expelled from Texas in 1835, then returned in force in 1836 and laid siege to a converted mission–fortress in San Antonio de Bexar, the Alamo. After a most heroic resistance, the 180-odd defenders were overwhelmed by a Mexican assault, and became martyrs to the cause of Texan Independence. Slain in the Alamo were two famous and beloved frontiersmen, Davy Crockett and James Bowie, whose deaths were seen in the United States as an almost sacrilegious act on the part of Santa Anna. Thousands of volunteers and dollars poured into Texas to join the 'war of liberation', but it was left to General Sam Houston and about 740 volunteers to meet Santa Anna at the Battle of San Jacinto (21 April 1836). The Texans, burning to avenge the massacres of the Alamo and Goliad (where some 300 Texans had been shot out of hand after surrendering), routed the Mexican army so completely that it literally ceased to exist, and Santa Anna was captured. Texas, declared an independent republic, was recognised by the U.S.A., a move which aroused intense feeling in Mexico and which, added to the American desire for continued expansion south and westwards, resulted in the U.S.–Mexican War of 1846–48.

NORTH AMERICAN UNIFORMS 1815–40 (Plates 43–46)

43. U.S.A.:

a) Sergeant, Grenadier Company, Infantry, 1827.

b) Officer, Artillery, 1827.

The bell-topped shako was adopted by the U.S. Army in 1821, this head-dress having a very marked outward curve near to the crown. It was worn by company officers and rank and file of all branches, being distinguished by the colour of the plume: white for infantry 'centre' companies, red for grenadiers, yellow for artillery and light infantry, white with red top for light artillery, and green for riflemen. The badge of an eagle grasping an olive branch and a sheaf of arrows, and chinscales, were of brass or white metal according to the branch, and the cords were similarly yellow or white (gold or silver for officers).

The 1821 pattern coatee had collar-lace of the branch distinctive colour, and shoulder-wings likewise; officers wore scaled wings with bullion fringes of the branch colour (silver or gold), which meant that the previous system of rank-designation by epaulette-design could not be used. Instead, commissioned grades were distinguished by metallic lace chevrons on the upper arms. N.C.O. rank was distinguished by lace chevrons of the branch colour on the forearm. As in European armies, musicians' uniforms were the most colourful of the army; those of the artillery, for example, wore scarlet coatees with lace and wings of the artillery's distinctive colour (yellow), with yellow cords and plumes on the shako. An interesting feature was the lack of lace on the breasts of all army coatees, which had lines of embroidery in the same colour as the coatee instead. Note also that the officers' sword illustrated was suspended from the belt by thin chains instead of the more usual leather slings.

44. U.S.A.:
a) Trooper, Dragoons, Service Dress, 1836.
b) Ordnance Sergeant, 1836.

The 'stovepipe' shako was adopted by infantry and artillery in 1832, here shown in the artillery version (the Ordnance Department had merged with the artillery in 1821). The infantry pattern had white metal badges and fittings, with a bugle-horn in place of the cannon-barrels, and a white plume. The height of the plume varied, but is thought to have been 12 inches high for senior N.C.O.s, 8 inches for sergeants and below, and of drooping cock-feathers for officers. The rank of Ordnance Sergeant was that of a senior N.C.O., one being assigned to every post or unit, responsible for the maintenance of arms and ammunition. The rank is indicated by the lace bars on the cuff, the sash, sword, and yellow worsted epaulettes with brass crescents.

Regular cavalry was revived in the U.S. Army in 1833, when the Regiment of Dragoons was raised. In full dress, the 'stovepipe' shako was worn, with a large brass star-shaped plate bearing a white metal eagle in the centre, and yellow cords (gold for officers) passing around the cap and looping on to the breast in two 'raquettes'. Plumes were of drooping white horsehair, with red intermixed for officers of field rank. This pattern of cap was later adopted by the mounted artillery, with red cords and plume.

The full dress coatee was of the same pattern as that worn by the Ordnance Sergeant, but had yellow collar and cuffs, with gold lace decoration for officers. N.C.O.s wore yellow worsted epaulettes and officers gold. The dragoon distinctive colour (yellow) was repeated in the double stripe on the officers' trousers. The figure illustrated shows the dragoon field uniform, consisting of a dark blue shell-jacket with yellow lace and the odd-shaped, leather forage cap worn by both foot and mounted branches of the army between 1833 and 1839, a plain head-dress without badges and so constructed that it could be folded flat for ease of carrying. In addition to the usual equipment used on active service (note that the waist-belt which supported the sword had an attached shoulder-belt as an extra support, similar to the later British 'Sam Browne' belt), dragoons often affected a number of unauthorised additions. Coloured bandanas worn around the neck or as a sun-shield to the back of the head were popular, and the trooper illustrated wears the trousers tucked into knee-boots instead of the more usual method of wearing the trousers over the boots. The company guidon carried by the trooper bears the word DRAGOONS, an addition ordered by Secretary of War Lewis Cass in 1833.

45. Mexico:
a) Sergeant, Batallon de Matamoros, 1836.
Texas:
b) Private, New Orleans Greys, 1836.

Of the scores – even hundreds – of

tiny (and not so tiny) volunteer units raised in the euphoric fervour of patriotism which swept over the United States during the War of Texan Independence, the two corps of New Orleans Greys were the most famous. Upholding the principles of the 1776 Revolution by assisting fellow-Americans, hundreds of idealists and a large number of adventurers and freebooters flocked to Texas to defend the rights of their brethren. The New Orleans Greys – dressed in hastily-produced uniforms from which they took their name – were one of the first units into Texas. One company was included in Colonel Fannin's force which was attacked on the Coleto River and forced to retire back to the Goliad mission from whence they had advanced; the inept Fannin surrendered and virtually his entire command was executed on the orders of the brutal Santa Anna. The other company of 'Greys' was included in the Alamo garrison when the mission fell; they also were annihilated to a man. At the time of the final assault, it was the Greys' proud light blue banner with emblazoned black eagle which flew over the Alamo, and now reposes in Mexico City where it was taken after the assault.

The Greys were in a ragged, ill-equipped state at the time of the siege of the Alamo, their quickly-produced uniforms having mostly fallen to pieces. Other volunteer corps wore home-made, civilian clothes with wide-brimmed hats or fur caps; although Colonel W. B. Travis (final garrison commander at the Alamo) had ordered a grey frock-coat and forage-cap from his tailor before the campaign, it wasn't completed in time and he died wearing home-made Texas jeans and carrying a shotgun. It was said that only one officer in the entire Texan army, Colonel Sydney Sherman, possessed a uniform at the time of San Jacinto, and that of his own devising. At San Jacinto, General Houston was dressed in 'an old black coat, a black velvet vest, a pair of snuff-coloured pantaloons, and dilapidated boots' with his trousers tucked in, 'his only badge of authority . . . a sword with a plated scabbard which he tied to his belt with buckskin thongs.' So amateur was the Texan army, in fact, that the only tune known to the two-man fife-and-drum band to play the Texan army into action was a popular love-song, 'Will You Come to the Bower I have Shaded for You?' Arms of the Texan army consisted of a few U.S.-issue muskets, shotguns, Kentucky 'long rifles' and the universal 'Bowie'-type knives. While the defenders of the Alamo were dying to prolong the life of the embattled Texas republic, the newly-elected government, instead of arranging for the arming and equipping of the Texan volunteers, concerned themselves with such vital matters as obtaining officially-headed notepaper and 'liquor fit for genteel men to drink.'

The Mexican army wore uniforms consciously based upon those of Imperial France, as befitted the troops of the self-styled 'Napoleon of the West' as Santa Anna delighted in calling himself. Although basically consisting of bell-topped shako, dark blue coat with coloured facings and often white trousers for summer wear, the uniforms of the expedition into Texas were an amalgam of Mexican military dress of the previous twenty years, frequently combined (from shortage of regulation equipment) with civilian items – simple peasant sandals instead of boots, for example. It is believed that some companies wore white cotton fatigue-suits with peasants' straw hats. The only regimental device on the uniform illustrated were the brass letters BM on the collar, signifying 'Batallon de Mata-moros'. The Mexican infantry was largely equipped with ancient British 'Brown Bess' flintlocks which many troops did not know how to fire, or at best fire from the hip, rendering already inaccurate weapons quite useless at more than ten yards; though some picked units were armed with British 'Baker' rifled muskets. But in general, as the whole expedition was dependent upon the most enormous bank overdraft, complicated by wholesale and unashamed theft of stores by the general staff, the Mexican army was ill-equipped, ill-trained, virtually un-supplied and on the extreme verge of starvation. For all their wretched condition, however, Santa Anna issued the most meticulous orders – in fact he did all his own staff work himself, his 'staff' being largely a sycophantic group of bandits. An example of his careful attention to detail was his order to the regiments assaulting the Alamo: they were to have bayonets ready-fixed, and the 'straps of the caps under the chin'.

For one whose hallmark was the magnificence of his uniforms, the 'Napoleon of the West' ended the

War of Texan Independence in an ignominious fashion – when captured after San Jacinto, Santa Anna was discovered up a tree, dressed in a dusty blue fatigue-jacket, battered leather cap, frayed linen trousers and red cloth slippers! Until released by his Texan captors, Santa Anna spent some time in Texas, whose in-habitants persisted in arranging impromptu lynching parties in his honour, though 'El Presidente' always managed to avoid being the main attraction.

46. Republic of Texas:
  a) **Officer,**
      Ordnance Dept,
      Service Dress
      (Winter), 1839.
  b) **1st Sergeant,**
      Infantry,
      Marching Order,
      1839.
  c) **Sergeant,**
      Marine Corps,
      Fatigue Dress, 1839.

The Republic of Texas provides an-other example of a new state without any existing uniform traditions, having to formulate a regulation dress. The basic uniform was copied from a combination of U.S. and Mexican styles, generally very ornate, and including a cavalry helmet not unlike the Mexican pattern, of black leather and brass with a horsehair crest. The infantry fatigue dress was based upon United States pattern, but included the tail-coat; the in-fantry full dress was like that worn by the Ordnance officer illustrated, but with silver lace and white shako-plume, with a white metal shako-plate in the form of a five-pointed star bearing the company letter, on a 'rayed' star-plate. The Texan 'Lone Star' emblem was much in use, on belt-plates, cap-plates, cartridge-boxes and as a stamp on regulation-issue weapons. Another unusual feature was the profusion of buttons on many full-dress uniforms – four around the top of each cuff and three down the rear seam of the cuff of infantry officers' coatees, for example (*Uniform of the Army*, published in Houston, 23 May 1839, the first Dress Regulations of the new republic).

The Marine Corps fatigue uniform illustrated was itself a very singular and attractive design, but the full dress even more so, consisting of infantry shako with oval brass plate bearing the 'Lone Star' and brass anchor badge, with brass chinscales; a sea-green jacket with yellow lace on the collar and cuff-flaps, yellow turn-backs, and yellow lace loops on the collar and cuff-flaps, with yellow fringed shoulder-rolls; sea-green trousers and grey gaiters, with white leather equipment and rectangular brass waist-belt plate bearing the 'Lone Star'. Arms for the forces of the Republic were sporadically-issued, and included a revolving-cylindered rifle used by the Marines, a most un-popular weapon due to its peculiarity of frequently igniting all chambers at once and exploding in the user's face! The marine sergeant illustrated is holding a privately-acquired, multi-barrelled 'Volley gun'.

COLONIAL CAMPAIGNS, 1815–50

The campaigns in the colonies – for Britain at least – provided the only chance of experiencing real action as different from the distasteful 'internal security' tasks which befell many armies. As with the French in Algeria and the Russians in the Caucasus, campaigning in India kept at least part of the British army in touch with the realities of active service.

From 1814–16 British troops in India were engaged in one of their most difficult campaigns, against the Nepalese hill-tribes, the Gurkhas. Despite a ferocious defence, strategic mountain-forts were captured one by one until General Ochterlony penetrated the Katmandu Valley and the Gurkhas sued for peace. Greatly impressed by the bravery of the British which matched their own courage, the Gurkhas furnished several battalions for British service and have served in a most outstanding manner ever since.

In 1817–18 a serious campaign was waged against the vast horde of Pindaris (outlaws and bandits) who caused utter mayhem in central and southern India, and against the Maratha chieftains who supported them. Sir Thomas Hyslop's 5,500-strong Army of the Deccan crushed one Maratha force of 35,000 at Mahidput (21 December 1817), and Lord Hasting's Grand Army hunted down the remainder.

In 1823 Burma launched an attack on India, prompting a declaration of war by Britain in March 1824. Major-General Campbell organised a 5,000-strong Anglo–Indian expedition force from the Andaman Islands, which landed and captured Rangoon in May. The disease-ravaged British, however, were surrounded by Maha Bandula's Burmese army, which on 1 December 1824 assaulted the city, only to be thrown back; two weeks later a British counter-attack broke the siege-lines and the Burmese retired. In February 1825 Campbell advanced up the Irrawaddy, supported by sixty boats manned by British sailors. Bandula attacked on 2 April, but his force was broken by fire from a British rocket-battery, and the Burmese were routed as Campbell advanced, Bandula being killed. Campbell, retiring into quarters at Prome for the monsoon season, was again surrounded, which siege was a duplicate of Rangoon; a Burmese attack in November was followed by a counter-attack which, in three days of intense fighting, destroyed the Burmese army and forced Burma to surrender, the victorious Campbell withdrawing in February 1826.

In 1825 Britain intervened in the Bhurtpore succession dispute; Lord Combermere's army invested the city and captured it after a desperate assault in January 1826. Following these repeated (and by now customary) British successes came disaster in the 1st Afghan War. In an attempt to block Russian advances in Afghanistan, a 21,000 strong British army invaded that country to support a puppet-ruler's claim to the throne in 1839, which was successfully accomplished. In 1841, however, the Afghans revolted, murdering both British political envoys in Kabul and surrounding General Elphinstone's garrison (November 1841). Two months later Elphinstone capitulated on the guarantee of safe passage to India for his 4,500 men and 12,000 civilians. The Afghans, led by the treacherous Akbar Khan, disregarded the terms of the agreement and ambushed the convoy in the Khyber Pass.

The sequence of events from the evacuation of Kabul was to prove the most shattering defeat of the British in India. As the incompetent Elphinstone approached the Jugdulluk Pass with his one British regiment (the 44th Foot) and various East India Company units, the Afghans harassed and sniped along the flanks, the column diminishing visibly. By the time that the Jugdulluk defile was reached, only 120 of the 44th and 25 artillerymen could be reckoned as an effective force, and thousands of camp-followers only made the situation worse. Jugdulluk was barricaded with thorn-bushes, and had to be stormed. Incredibly, the little party forced their way through, though from Elphinstone's original 4,500 fighting men all that now remained were 20 officers and 45 soldiers. A dozen officers rode ahead towards Jallalabad and its British garrison, but the remainder were unable to proceed further and made their last stand on 13 January 1842 at Gandamak. Only half a dozen were captured, and none escaped. The redoubtable Subedar Sita Ram was taken prisoner by the Afghans shortly before the final assault, and described the remnant of the 44th: they 'fought like gods, not men, but numbers prevailed against them . . .'

Of the twelve who had ridden ahead from Gandamak, only one reached the safety of Jallalabad, the now-famous Dr William Brydon, who became the subject of Lady Butler's emotive painting, 'Remnants of an Army'. Sadly for legend, Dr Brydon, so long billed as the 'sole survivor' of Elphinstone's force, was one of a considerable number who eventually escaped or survived captivity, but his ride to Jallalabad is no less of an epic for that. Even today the inhabitants of Gandamak point out the 'black rocks' around which the British died, but in Britain itself

146

the retreat from Kabul is generally forgotten. Later in 1842 Sir George Pollock stormed into Afghanistan, relieving the beleagured garrison of Jallalabad and wreaking vengeance for the Gandamak massacre. But, anxious not to lose more troops in the inhospitable mountains, the British evacuated the area and Akbar Khan's father, Dost Mohammed, was allowed to resume the throne from which he had been originally deprived.

Following the 1st Afghan War and the friction it had caused between the Baluch rulers of Sind and the British, the British Residency at Hyderabad was stormed by 8,000 Baluchis in February 1843. Marching in relief of the tiny besieged garrison, General Sir Charles Napier with 2,800 men defeated 30,000 Baluchis at Miani (17 February), made a formidable forced march through barren country and in March relieved Hyderabad. In his whirlwind campaign Napier marched 600 miles, fought two major battles and numerous minor actions and with no more than 5,000 men defeated over 60,000 natives. The conquest of Sind stabilised India's western frontier, secured the Indus, and prompted Napier's famous one-word dispatch announcing his victory: 'Peccavi' (I have sinned)!

Continued friction between the British and the Sikhs of the Punjab resulted in a Sikh invasion of British India in December 1845, but their first advance was halted by Sir Hugh Gough at Mudki (18 December). Three days later Gough – with the British Governor-General Sir Henry Hardinge serving in a subordinate capacity – attacked a well-entrenched Sikh army of 50,000 at Ferozeshah. The action was complicated by the fact that it was not clear who was giving orders to the British force, Commander-in-Chief or Governor-General, and several assaults were beaten off before the British captured the position and repelled a counter-attack on the following day. One of the bitterest struggles in Indian history, Ferozeshah cost Gough 2,400 men and the Sikhs at least 10,000, causing the Sikhs to withdraw back over the River Sutlej whence they had come.

Another Sikh army, raiding in British territory, skirmished with a British force under Sir Harry Smith at Ludhiana (21 January 1846); Smith attacked a week later and smashed the Sikhs at Aliwal in another brutal, no-quarter action. In February Gough himself crossed the Sutlej and stormed a Sikh position at Sobraon, which ended the war – Punjab becoming a British protectorate.

Of short duration, the war had been one of the bloodiest ever fought in India, due to the valiant character of the Sikh nation and their well-trained and organised army. So well was it equipped and uniformed, in fact, that it was said the only way of distinguishing a Sikh unit from a British sepoy corps in the confusion of battle was that the Sikhs wore black or brown cross-belts, and the British white.

A fact not generally known is that the Sikh army was trained to a considerable degree by Europeans, either foreign mercenaries or deserters from the British or Company's forces. At Sobraon, for example, two mercenary officers were present in the Sikh army, one Hurbon (a Spaniard) and his French colleague Moulton; and Subedar Sita Ram tells of an incident which occurred during the heat of the battle when a 'Sikh' cried out to a British private for mercy, 'a thing no Sikh had ever been known to do', and then spoke in English. The British private pulled off the man's turban and jacket, to reveal a European deserter who had turned against his comrades by taking service in the Sikh army. A party of British infantry kicked and bayonetted him to death with the greatest contempt and violence.

Knowing how near they had come to victory, the Sikhs tried again in 1848–49 when the Punjab rose in revolt, with the Sikh government at first attempting to suppress it and then turning on the British themselves. General Whish laid siege to Multan while Gough again invaded the Punjab. Gough, checked at Ramnagar (22 November 1848) at first decided to wait for Whish to take Multan, but then advanced independently. Meeting the Sikhs at Chilianwalah (13 January 1849) – when both armies attacked at once – Gough lost fewer men than the Sikhs but the sanguinary battle was in reality drawn. His replacement by Napier ordered, Gough moved before the orders arrived, his army reinforced by Whish (and the Sikhs by Dost Mohammed of Afghanistan). The Battle of Gujerat on 21 February finally broke the Sikh resistance for trifling British loss, and the Punjab was annexed in the following month.

British operations were not confined to India; in 1839 disagreement between British merchants and the Chinese government (particularly regarding the importation of opium) led to Chinese action against the European community. An expedition of 4,000 British and East India Company troops under Sir Hugh Gough arrived in Chinese waters, capturing the Bogue Forts and Canton (24 May 1841). Despite unseaworthy transports and lack of supplies, the disease-ravaged British continued coastal operations which culminated in the fall of Chingkiang (21 July 1842) and China sued for peace.

In Africa, conflict with native tribes continued throughout the period, both between the Boer settlers and the natives, between British and natives, and ultimately British and Boers. Notable actions occurred at Blood River (16 December 1838) when a Boer force decisively defeated a Zulu army under Dingaan, at Magango (January 1840), when a Boer–Zulu alliance overthrew Dingaan, and at Boomplaats (29 August 1848) when Sir Harry Smith's British victory culminated six years of Anglo–Boer conflict. Harry Smith was involved in an amazing incident in the suppression of the 3rd Kaffir War (1834–36), when that iron veteran of the Peninsula and Waterloo led a small detachment from Cape Town to Graham's Town, a distance of 600 miles, in less than six days, a scarcely credible feat of endurance over the most difficult terrain.

Between 1824–27 the 1st Ashanti War was fought in West Africa, with initial British reverses being turned into victory; and in 1846–47 a sharp campaign against the Kaffirs in South Africa silenced native protests about increasing European colonisation. Other British colonies were peaceful, except for two minor revolts (the Papineau and Mackenzie rebellions) in Canada, and the 1st Maori War in New Zealand (1843–48), which included some hard skirmishing and a guerrilla war before the natives were subdued.

The other major sphere of colonial activity was the French invasion of Algeria in 1830, following repeated blockading and bombardment in an effort to check the depredations of Algerian pirates. Algiers was captured in July 1830 by Marshal de Bourmont's 37,000 men, but the campaign dragged on against a skilled native leader, Abd el Kader, the self-appointed defender of Islam and a man of remarkably chivalrous disposition. The Treaty of Tafna (June 1837) brought an uneasy peace, but the French stormed Constantine in October, the city having resisted French attacks for a year; the French commander, Marshal Damremont, was killed in the assault. Claiming this as a treaty-violation Abd el Kader took the field again.

With the French army now commanded by the dynamic Marshal Bugeaud, new tactics were adopted; 'flying columns', as mobile as the Berbers they hunted, were sent out from fixed bases and had a decisive effect; in May 1843 the Duc d'Aumale with less than 2,000 men surprised Abd el Kader's 40,000 at Smala and utterly routed them. Driven into Morocco, Abd el Kader with 45,000 men were attacked by Bugeaud himself at Isly (14 August 1844); Bugeaud's small force, using a 'square' formation devised by the Marshal and known as the 'boar's head', attacked and overran the Arab camp. It proved decisive;

although Abd el Kader did not surrender until December 1847, French control of Algeria was assured.

As a result of colonial campaigning, military uniforms took on a more functional and climatically more suitable aspect, with virtual 'fatigue dress' becoming the established uniform for active service; plates 49, 51 and 64 illustrate how these 'colonial' fashions were carried over into European service. The British in India also produced full dress costume of great magnificence, frequently incorporating native items of dress in the uniforms of European officers (undeniably adding to the overall romanticism of the period), while native soldiers of the East India Company's forces (officially the only 'British' regiments in India were those actually belonging to the Crown) were dressed in an often-incongruous mixture of current British uniform, pseudo-Indian items (such as peakless shakos intended to resemble turbans) and genuine 'native' features such as sandals and beads around the neck!

The French campaigns in Algeria were begun by troops wearing standard infantry uniform (see Plate 38) with white linen shako-covers, but soon evolved into a more suitable 'tenue d'Afrique', which included a cloth-bodied shako-type head-dress known as a 'casquette d'Afrique' (the forerunner of the famous and ultimately world-wide 'képi'), and the habit of wearing the greatcoat with skirts turned back to allow free movement of the legs, without the tunic underneath, a style to be seen even in World War I. The strangulating constructions of the 1830's were replaced by more functional equipment, including the wearing of the cartridge-box at the front of the waist. And in the exotically-costumed 'African' regiments – Zouaves, Chasseurs d'Afrique, Spahis – the French set a style which was to be copied extensively in North America and even by the British West India Regiments. A description of the semi-native costume originally worn by the Zouaves (the name coming from the Algerian Zouaoua tribe who supplied troops to aid the French) was given as: 'tricolour turban with an aigrette, blue Turkish jacket, embroidered in gold, red mameluke trousers, with gold trimmed pockets, silk sash full of pistols, and a curved sabre'; this costume was worn initially by the French officers also, but soon replaced by conventional European dress when 'they found these disguises so grotesque (that) they hurriedly abandoned them . . .'

The French campaigns in North Africa speeded the development of tactics (the 'flying column', for example) and weapons; at a time when the British were hesitantly considering the introduction of smoothbore percussion muskets, the French were experimenting with weapons technically years ahead. Captain Delvigne, for example, designed a rifle which achieved a great reputation in Algeria. The Duke of Orléans equipped a battalion of Chasseurs d'Afrique with Delvigne's gun, and on one reconnaissance was much provoked by an Arab sheikh making threatening gestures some 650 yards away. The Duke called to his escort that he would give five francs to any man who could shoot the Arab, whereupon a Chasseur stepped forward, aimed his Delvigne rifle and laid the sheik dead upon the spot!

COLONIAL UNIFORMS 1815–50 (Plates 47–51)

47. Danish West Indies:
   a) Private,
      Regular Infantry,
      Service Dress (Summer),
      1837.
   b) Lieutenant,
      Regular Infantry,
      Full Dress (Winter),
      1826.

Relieved of the necessity of adapting uniforms for the rigours of campaigning, the Danish garrisons of the peaceful islands of St Thomas, St Croix and St John wore colourful uniforms which conformed in some respects to regular Danish uniform but also reflected the romantic spirit of the beautiful islands in which they served.

The 1826 winter uniform illustrated was replaced in summer by a white coatee and white trousers; officers (unlike home-based Danish regimental officers) wore fringed epaulettes, their rank indicated by the number of lace rosettes worn above the cuff; one for 2nd lieutenants, two for 1st lieutenants and three for captains. Other ranks at this period wore black felt 'stovepipe' hats with

brim, white metal badge, white pompom and mixed red-and-yellow cords; their uniform was like that of the officers but with blue shoulder-straps and unlaced trousers, and black leather equipment; white trousers were also worn in winter full dress as well as with the white jacket in summer. The 1837 uniform – including the tall and unusually-shaped czapka – was also worn by officers, but with the lace worn on the upper edge of the collar, with silver-laced pouch-belt and fringeless epaulettes, and gold-and-crimson sash with heavy tassels. Officers' czapkas were of the same pattern as those of the rank and file, but with tall white plume rising from the red cockade bearing a silver cross, large gilt 'sunburst' plate bearing silver coat-of-arms, silver chinscales and gold cords. As before, blue trousers could be worn with this uniform.

In addition to the regular infantry illustrated, there also existed militia units, wearing varied costume; in 1816, for example, the 'Prince's Life Squadron' wore a uniform virtually identical to that worn in the Peninsular War by the British 95th Rifles, officers wearing 'stovepipe' shako with green cords, green dolman with black facings and hussar braid, silver shoulder-chains, crimson-and-gold barrelled sashes and grey overalls with black leather reinforcing and braiding, the only real difference being in the large silver shako-plate, the white-over-red upright plume and the straight-bladed sword with mixed gold and crimson knot.

At the same date, the St Thomas Land Militia (again for officers) wore a black 'round hat' with gold loop and white-over-red plume (like the British Royal Marines), a dark blue jacket with rows of buttons on the breast, red facings with gold lace loop and epaulettes, white breeches and black Hessian boots. Militia uniforms followed the same 'natural progression' as did all European costume; in 1829 for example, the St Croix Militia wore bell-topped shako with white lace and cords, dark green jacket with white lace and piping and white trousers. Their cartridge-boxes bore the same cross device (on a crowned, white metal disc) as did the czapka-cockades of the regular infantry illustrated.

48. Indian Army:
a) Sepoy,
   Nasseri Battalion,
   1816.
b) Trumpeter,
   Skinner's Horse
   (1st Bengal Local Horse),
   1828.

By giving the British such a tremendous fight in the Nepalese War, it was obvious that the Gurkhas were superb soldiers, characterised by their motto 'Kaphar hunnu bhanda marnu ramro' (it is better to die than be a coward'). The first Gurkha units in British service were formed in 1815, both Nasseri and Sirmoor battalions wearing a semi-'rifle', semi-native uniform, originally with red facings but from 1816 (at least in the case of the Sirmoor) black. The wearing of the kukri, the fearsome and traditional native sword–knife which has an almost mystic attachment to the Gurkhas, was personally sanctioned by Sir David Ochterlony: 'Each man to retain and wear his kookrey in a leather waist-belt of the pattern which has been approved'. The exact construction of the first head-dress is uncertain, but appears from contemporary pictures to have been a flat-topped cap with a turban wound around. Initially the Gurkhas were armed with muskets, until a sufficient number of smaller (and therefore more manageable by the little Nepalese hillmen!) fuzils were made available.

If Gurkha reputation was formidable in 1815, it increased a thousandfold under British control. An early example of typical Gurkha courage is found in the despatch written by Colonel Sebright Mawbey, commander of the forces investing Kalunga after the death of Sir Rollo Gillespie in the first assault. When the fortress was evacuated by the Gurkha troops of Bulbudder Sing, the British found a wounded native officer (Bulbudder's aide) in the ruins of the fort. This man, 'finding that the wound would not put him to death, he abused both Officers and Men in the grossest terms in hopes that, they would by that means shoot him – but finding that, this would have no effect on their feelings – he beat his head against the Stones in the hope of putting an end to his existence – which all failing, he requested fire to warm himself, & when left by the Sepoys, he took an opportunity of throwing the whole of it on his breast – which was no sooner discovered than it was removed – he has, however, since died . . . .'

It is fitting that Plate 48 should be shared by a Gurkha (arguably the best soldier in the world), and a member of the most famous British–Indian regiment, ultimately Skinner's Horse (1st Bengal Lancers), the figure being taken from a painting of a durbar by a contemporary Persian artist.

Skinner's Horse had its origin in a corps of 'irregular horse' raised by a half-caste English officer, James Skinner, in 1803, which became the 1st Bengal Local Horse in 1823. Though pictures of 1817 show them wearing flat red turbans and yellow robes, by 1825 their dress had become more 'uniform', still retaining the distinctive yellow colour which they wore throughout their existence. The 'uniform' of the period shown consisted of a metal, Persian-style helmet with nasal-bar and a 'brush-type' plume for native officers, with a long yellow garment known as an 'alkalak' (embroidered with native design in metallic thread for officers), with either green or red trousers, and a short red jacket with black fur trimming in a similar pattern for all ranks. Arms consisted of native swords

(tulwars), ancient matchlock muskets, and lances with either narrow red pennons or occasionally bunches of coloured ribbon below the head. The figure illustrated is particularly interesting as it shows that despite the Indo–Persian nature of the uniform, the European 'reversed colours' fashion for musicians was used (i.e. red alkalaks and yellow jackets), with dark (probably green) tight trousers. European officers wore the old light dragoon uniform replaced in the British army in 1812 – Tarleton helmet with leopardskin turban and bearskin crest, red dolman with silver hussar-style braiding and white breeches, though apparently by 1830 the dolman was dark blue with red facings (and silver braid). On occasion, however, European officers wore ornate versions of the native dress, even including the Persian helmet with gilded fittings.

49. Indian Army:
  a) Sergeant, Light Company, 28th Bengal Native Infantry, 1846.
  b) Corporal, 1st Madras (European) Fusiliers, Service Dress, 1846.
  c) Band-Sergeant, Madras Native Infantry, 1846.

This plate shows variations of the Indian infantry uniform. The Havildar (sergeant) of the 28th Bengal (taken from an 1846 Ackermann print) shows the combination of European and native styles. In most respects (apart from the odd green wing-fringes, worn by a few British regiments, and the inverted chevrons), the uniform might be worn by a British unit, except for the peakless shako characteristic of Indian troops of this period. As in the British army, blue-black trousers were worn in winter. The shako could be worn with a plain black or white cover with ornaments removed, or replaced by a white-covered 'pillbox' undress cap for active service.

Native commissioned officers wore their own version of the peakless shako (the design of which varied considerably between units) and uniforms similar in style and decoration to those of British infantry officers, with the same 'company' distinctions (wings and green plumes for light companies, etc.). European officers in native units wore uniforms which duplicated current British styles exactly, given the various regimental distinctions, of course. Native troops wore this 'Europeanised' costume from the 1820's, until which time their dress had included more oriental items such as dome-topped turban–shakos and short trousers; even 'war-paint' was not officially forbidden until 1840! The marker flag illustrated is another unusual item shown in the original print, bearing the regimental number in gold letters.

Drummers and musicians were generally of mixed blood, and as such the official regulations prohibiting the wear of some 'European' items by natives did not apply; many musicians, for example, were allowed to wear peaked head-dress, a distinction reserved for those with some European ancestry. As in the British army, regimental bands adopted exotic and colourful costume, as shown by the senior N.C.O. of Madras Infantry, taken from another Ackermann print. As late as 1846 drummers were wearing 'reversed colours' – a Martens print of that date shows a drummer of the 65th Bengal wearing a yellow jacket with scarlet facings and white lace, brass shoulder-scales, and scarlet bell-topped shako with gold cords and white hanging plume. The 35th Bengal in 1848 wore white coat with crimson collar, cuffs and plastrons, light red trousers and 'Kilmarnock'-type cap, while the 28th Bengal wore an even more splendid dress – including czapka with brass plate, red cloth top and drooping white plume, double-breasted white coatee with green collar and cuffs, gold lace and epaulettes for all ranks, crimson sashes for all and red trousers.

The European regiments of the East India Company formed the élite of the Company's forces; taken into the British army after the Mutiny, the regiment illustrated ultimately became the 1st Bn Royal Dublin Fusiliers. The regiment wore a uniform like that of current British regulations, with facings successively French grey, white, and on becoming Fusiliers in 1843, dark blue. Another distinguishing feature peculiar to the regiment was the red ball-tuft on the shako. The figure illustrated, however (based on a sketch by Captain Ryves) shows the modified uniform worn on campaign, the shako being enclosed in a white linen cover, the tail-less undress jacket worn with collar turned down (note the unusual blue wings bearing white grenade badge), and the issue boots replaced by more comfortable, light native sandals. Capt. Ryves showed the troops carrying their leather stocks on the end of their muskets! The same artist portrayed the drum-major wearing a fur fusilier cap with white plume, gold lace and epaulettes on the jacket, and the more usual white trousers. The fact that the subject of Capt. Ryves' picture was shown fording a stream explains the rolled-up trousers and bare feet!

50. Indian Army:
   a) **Officer,**
      1st Madras Light Cavalry,
      1848.
   b) **Officer, 6th Bengal**
      Irregular Cavalry, 1849.

While native sowars (cavalry troopers) wore uniforms of traditional Indian styles (alkalaks and turbans) European officers wore either British-style light cavalry dress or a 'Euro-peanised' native costume. The officer of the 6th Bengal Cavalry illustrated is an example of the latter, wearing a native alkalak and using red, yellow and blue saddle-cloth and tufts of the same colour on the harness, but with the European sabretache (bearing VI over a crescent over the letters BIC in script) and the distinctive black leather plumed helmet, reputedly an honour conferred by the King of Prussia to commemorate the visit of Prince Waldemar to Sind and styled on those of the Prussian army. Native ranks wore large, flat blue turbans.

The other figure shows the typical British dragoon dress as worn by the 1st Madras Light Cavalry, taken (like the other figure) from an Ackermann print. Of 'cavalry grey' (a shade which varied from a true light grey to a bright blue) this uniform was one of the most magnificent ever worn by an Indian army unit, and included the Maltese Cross shaped shako-plate as worn in the British army. British officers of Indian light cavalry wore a dress which was without question the most magnificent worn by any army at any period. In the years up to the Indian Mutiny, virtually every imaginable style of uniform – hussar dress with shako or busby, light dragoon with shako, dragoon-style with crested helmets (huge red woollen crests on black helmetsfor the Madras corps in 1839), metal helmets with flowing manes (again frequently red), czapkas with enormous feather panaches, and with dolmans of sky blue, grey, 'bright' blue, scarlet, dark green, native-style alkalaks, shell-jackets and furred pelisses. Native ranks, while having a simpler dress and either turbans or dome-topped shako–turbans, nevertheless, reflected the lace-covered glory of their officers. The native regiments included some redoubtable characters –– for example, Subedar-Major Mir Sher Ali of the 8th Bengal Light Cavalry, who was killed charging with his regiment at Ramnagar (1848), at which time he had sixty years' service and was seventy-eight years old!

51. Britain:
   a) **Officer,**
      3rd Light Dragoons,
      Sikh War, 1845.
   b) **Private,**
      Light Company, 29th Foot,
      Sikh War, 1845–46.

A sharp contrast–to the magnificent but impractical uniforms described in Plate 50 is provided by the dress worn by the British army actually engaged in carving out an Empire and keeping the peace in that part already absorbed in the East India Company's holdings. The 3rd Light Dragoons officer is shown wearing what was virtually the regulation undress uniform (the full dress pattern is shown in Plate 27), with the shako covered by a tropical linen cover with attached neck-protector. Although troopers often wore the double-breasted full-dress jacket with covered shako, most officers preferred the single-breasted shell-jacket with a row of 'dummy' buttons on the front (the garment fastening with hooks-and-eyes), worn with the plain, undress sabretache. The shako was on occasion replaced by a forage-cap with white cover and neckcloth as worn by the other figure in this plate.

The shell-jacket had been worn for a number of years prior to the Sikh Wars (see Plate 25), during which the eye-witness descriptions were taken which form the basis for the figure of the 29th Foot. The garment was characterised by its plainness, devoid of lace and with plain facings. Only the brass bugle-horn on the front of the cap-cover (with attached neckcloth) worn above the regimental number indicated the wearer as a member of the light company. In addition to the light blue cotton trousers illustrated, plain white and blue-black trousers were also worn during these campaigns. Forage-cap design varied between corps; some wore caps with a padded upper

section, like those of the U.S. Army (Plates 57 and 58).

One contemporary painting of the 31st Foot at Ferozeshah shows the latter type with the letters XXXI painted in black on the front of the cap-cover, apparently worn without neck-guard; the same painting shows the 31st in plain red shell-jackets and blue-black trousers. An item peculiar to the 29th was a star-shaped brass badge on the flap of the cartridge-box. Officers frequently wore shell-jackets fastened by hooks-and-eyes, totally devoid of buttons, and often a plain red, double-breasted jacket with turned-down lapels very similar in style to a modern lounge suit, worn over the shell-jacket. It should be noted that along with everything else, the trousers faded in the bright Indian sun to an indistinct greyish hue. Leather equipment, frequently left unwhitened, took on a buff to light brown colour. Some regiments, however, apparently did not adopt the peaked forage cap; the 16th Lancers charged at Aliwal apparently wearing their czapkas with white covers and probably white trousers. Reputedly they even carried their lance-pennons, which after the charge (according to regimental tradition) were so soaked with blood that they had to be cleaned and were ever afterwards 'crimped' to commemorate the event.

Officers frequently equipped themselves with non-regulation and even 'native' garments; in the colder regions of India the fur 'poshteen' overcoat was popular, and at least one famous incident arose from its use. At the end of the retreat from

Kabul, when the last remnant of Elphinstone's force was overwhelmed at Gandamak, Captain Souter of the 44th had tied the Regimental Colours around his body, under his poshteen, in an effort to prevent their capture by the Afghans. In defending himself in the last assault, Souter's coat came open revealing the embroidered flag and the Afghans, presuming that Souter must be a man of great importance to wear so magnificent a waistcoat, spared his life in the hopes of a large ransom. He was the only officer to survive the last attack.

It is also interesting to note a most unusual item used in the Nepalese War by Lieutenant John Shipp of the 87th Foot. Shipp, a remarkable character (he was a workhouse boy who rose from the ranks and was twice court-martialled) met a Gurkha chief (one 'Khissna Rhannah Bahader') in single combat. The chief (who dressed in a 1790's British general's coat!) was eventually slain by Shipp, who then 'took his sword, gold crescent, turban, chain and large shield; this last I sported on my arm for the rest of the action, and it was lucky I did so, for it was bullet proof and saved me a severe wound'.

The 3rd Light Dragoons (illustrated) had a service-record in India literally second to none; this magnificent regiment lost no fewer than 289 men and 364 horses in the 1st Sikh War alone.

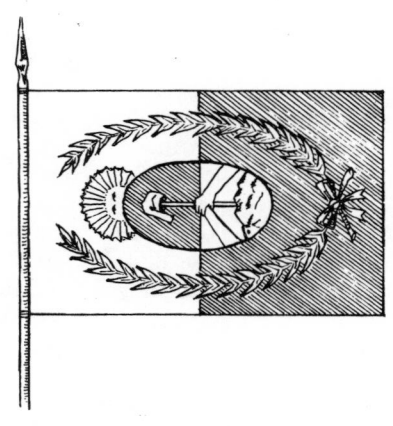

OPERATIONS IN EUROPE, 1840–48

Europe became involved in the 2nd Turko–Egyptian War (1839–41) when it appeared that the Ottoman Empire – long the 'sick man of Europe' – was about to collapse completely. With fears of Russian expansion if Turkey disintegrated, the great powers (except France) decided to intervene. An Anglo–Austrian fleet cut the sea communications of the Egyptian army in Syria and their homeland, and the war was ended when Syria was abandoned by the Egyptians, after British bombardment, invasion and occupation of Beirut and Acre.

Trouble flared again in Spain, when General Espartero led a revolt which drove Queen Isabella from her throne in 1840. Espartero suppressed monarchist risings in 1841 and 1842, but the Civil War ended when General Narvaez led a successful counter-rebellion which restored Isabella to her throne. Espartero escaped and was to play a significant rôle in the 1854 revolution. A brief revolt in Greece (1843) forced King Otto I to grant constitutional government, and in 1845 even Switzerland felt the wind of civil conflict, when the Swiss Federal Assembly decided to use force against seven rebellious Catholic cantons. The brief 'Sonderbund' war which followed two years later – because of which Switzerland remained undivided – was fought for almost solely religious motives (and with trifling loss of life) and was therefore a strange anomaly in a world torn by international power-politics and internal republican dissent.

In 1846 the independent city-state of Cracow – all that remained of an independent Poland – began a local insurrection against Austria, intended to be another general Polish rising. It was rapidly crushed by Austrian troops and Cracow absorbed into the Austro–Hungarian empire. With one insurrectionalist movement after another, events were leading to the climax of 1848, when the forces of dissent – democrat, republican or whatever – made a concerted effort to topple the existing order of Europe.

In the early 1840's the trend towards a simplification of uniforms was accelerating, due to the colonial wars and the considerable number of 'security' operations inside Europe, but the change was still very slow. Two national styles were to dominate world-wide uniform-design from the late 1840's, those of France and Prussia, and each was to epitomise a different school of political thought and military theory. The German style represented the harshly-disciplined, precision-drilled armies of conservatism, and the looser, more comfortable French clothing the more carefree style of independent movement and progressive tactics. Obviously, the distinctions were not clear-cut and were at times downright misleading, but it is significant that when Britain raised her Rifle Volunteers in 1859–60, a body who were to act independently as skirmishers without the restrictive tactics of the line, the loose French uniform and cloth képi was the obvious choice for the vast majority of volunteer corps.

EUROPEAN UNIFORMS 1840–48 (Plates 52–56)

52. Bavaria:
    a) **Colonel,**
       1st Cuirassiers
       (Prince Charles of
       Bavaria), 1835.
Prussia:
    b) **Officer,**
       Guard Hussars,
       1845.

This plate illustrates two old-style uniforms made without any concessions to efficiency. A notable feature of the Prussian Guard Hussar costume (while conforming to ordinary hussar pattern) is the 'Guard Star' (in reality the Star of the Order of the Black Eagle) worn on the busby and pouch, consisting of a black enamelled eagle on a silver star, with a gilt laurel-wreath and motto, SUUM CUIQUE.

The officer of the 1st Bavarian Cuirassiers is based upon a lithograph by Krauss of Munich, showing the regimental colonel, Prince Charles of Bavaria. The fur-crested helmet and cuirass were worn with the traditional Bavarian medium-blue uniform; the cuirass was adopted in 1815 and the helmet shown replaced an earlier model when the 1st and 2nd Cuiras-

siers and the Garde du Corps were amalgamated in 1825 to form the new 1st Cuirassiers. The original white breeches were replaced by blue overalls with red piping between 1829 and 1832, the wide red stripe replacing the piping in 1834. Besides a generally plainer uniform, other ranks of the regiment had a different head-dress; of the same shape, it had an all-brass crest and no turban, this latter (with its inset foliage-sprays) being reserved for officers. The print on which this figure is based also shows the regimental band; wearing ordinary other ranks' uniforms, they are shown mounted but without the cuirass, their single-breasted coatees having silver buttons and red piping down the front opening. The bandmaster has N.C.O.s' silver lace around the top of the cuffs and top and front of the collar. Horse-furniture was of cream sheepskin with medium blue cloth edging, officers having a square-cut medium blue shabraque, edged with silver lace and bearing a crowned royal cypher in the rear corners, this pattern being adopted in 1830. In the original, Prince Charles is shown wearing the ribband of the Order of St Hubert, crimson with light green edges.

53. Prussia:
a) Trooper, 3rd Dragoons, 1843.
b) Officer, 2nd Schützen (Rifle) Bn, Summer Dress, 1843.

In 1843 the Prussian army underwent a complete change of uniform. The spiked leather helmet, at this period very tall and with square-cut peak, was copied from the original Russian design. With the 'pickelhaube' (spiked helmet) came the flared-skirted tunic and soon afterwards new infantry equipment, probably copied from French patterns and consisting of two side braces supporting a waist-belt, from which hung an ammunition pouch on either side of the front. The new helmet was worn with a plume in parade dress by some corps instead of the spike, the plate being made in the shape of an eagle for all except Guard troops, who retained their 'Guard Star'; the national cockade was worn behind the chinscale bosses. The tunic – shown here in the colouring of the 2nd Schützen (Rifle) Battalion – retained the old dark blue colour for infantry, with red facings and coloured shoulder-straps bearing the regimental number. Drummers (as before) wore red wings of the 'swallow's nest' variety; it should be noted that in all cases only the front half of the collar was of the facing colour. Though rifle units wore round cuffs, infantry had cuff-patches. Trousers were white for summer and charcoal grey with red

piping for winter. An interesting feature of officers' uniforms was the method of wearing the sword; the tunics had such widely-flared skirts that the sword had to pass through the tunic, only the hilt protruding from under the skirt just in front of the knot and hanging tassels of the sash. Officers were further distinguished by laced shoulder-straps with gilt crescents.

The tunic and spiked helmet were adopted by all Prussian cavalry except for hussars and lancers, some cavalry helmets being made of metal instead of leather. The dragoon illustrated has the traditional light blue uniform with coloured facings; cuirassiers wore the tunic laced around the collar and cuffs and down the front as before, and with a curious welt around the armholes of the tunic. Their helmets were metal. Artillery wore infantry-pattern helmets with dark blue tunics faced black, with cuffs cut like those of rifle units. Even the Garde du Corps took the spiked helmet, of brass with the spike replaced by a metal eagle for parade and gala occasions, when a scarlet 'supreveste' (a waist-length tabard) with white lace and the Guard Star embroidered on the front was worn over the white tunic. Hussars retained the dolman and pelisse until 1855, worn with a busby or a shortened version of the old 'mirliton' cap. Uhlans (lancers) continued to wear the czapka and plastroned jackets until 1853 when the tunic was adopted. Landwehr units took the pickelhaube and tunic at the same time as the regular army, the tunic being unpiped down the front and the helmet bearing the distinctive landwehr cross badge.

This uniform was extensively copied from the outset; the Swedish army, for example, introduced a 'kask' like the Prussian helmet but with rounded peak and the Swedish triple-crowns badge on the front; their whole uniform (of the infantry, for example) was dark blue, with piping around the cuffs, down the tunic-front and on the trouser-seams; collar-fronts and lapels were faced in the colour of the military district. Even the small army raised by Schleswig-Holstein was wearing the Prussian uniform by 1848 (with eagle-shaped helmet-plate, coloured facings and lighter blue trousers), and another example of the widely-copied Prussian style is shown in Plate 60.

54. France:
   a) Trooper,
      Paris Republican Guard,
      1848.
   b) Grenadier,
      Infantry, 1845.
In the mid-1840's French uniform changed radically, partly as a result of the experiences in North Africa. In 1843 a shako based on the 'casquette d'Afrique' was ordered, and was actually introduced in February 1844. The original version had no plate, bearing the regimental number on the bottom band, but in March 1845 a plate bearing a stamped number was authorised. Grenadiers and voltigeurs continued to wear double-pompoms of red and yellow respectively; for wet weather waterproof covers with the regimental number painted on the front were

provided, these sometimes being worn with the pompom (for example, a Raffet print of the 33rd Regiment in Italy in 1849 shows this).

The 1845 regulations introduced a three-quarter length tunic with flared skirts; the uniform illustrated (taken from a contemporary print) is unusual as it shows a 'transitional' uniform, including the 1844 shako (prior to the issue of the plate) with a version of the new tunic. Long-service distinctions in the form of chevrons were worn on the sleeves as before. The new tunic was accompanied by a new design of equipment, in which the brass-hilted 'Roman' sword, bayonet and cartridge-box were carried on the waistbelt, supported by straps attached to the pack-straps and fastened by brass clips; the waistbelt had a new clip-type fastener. The greatcoat was officially grey, but became bluer in tone, and was worn with the epaulettes; it was usually carried rolled on top of the knapsack in a waterproof case, the tunic being carried here when the greatcoat was worn. Contemporary prints show both white and black leather equipment, often modified on campaign to the wearer's preference; though officially positioned at the rear, the cartridge-box continued to be worn at the front on active service.

The other figure (from a Victor Adam lithograph) illustrates 'political' uniform; based on a romanticised idea of working dress, the képi, scarves and loose trousers all symbolised the 'democratic' political thought as different from the tighter, 'establishment' style of dress. More important, though, was the fact that it was both distinctive and quickly-produced. The Paris Municipal Guard was dismissed in 1848 following the Revolution, and replaced by the Garde Républicaine de l'Hôtel de Ville, a 600-strong volunteer corps; this was itself disbanded on 27 May 1848 and replaced by the Paris Republican Guard. The early uniform illustrated was later replaced by a more conventional military style.

55. Spain:

a) Trooper,
1st Calatrava Lancers,
1845.

b) Trumpeter,
1st King's Cuirassiers,
1845.

In Spain, the British-style uniforms worn at the end of the Napoleonic Wars were replaced by costume of marked French influence. Infantry wore bell-topped shakos and later the tall, slightly tapering model, with blue uniforms. Despite regimental and national features (insignia, badges and cockade) Spanish uniforms became so French in design (including red trousers worn by some units) that in some cases at first glance there might have been confusion as to the nationality of the Spanish soldier! Light infantry wore green uniforms, but other distinguishing features (shako-trimming, etc.) followed the French style – red for grenadiers, etc.

The two cavalry uniforms (from lithographs by Victor Adam) are similarly based on French patterns, but with Spanish features. The ordinary uniform of the 1st Cuirassiers consisted of brass helmet of the pattern worn by the lancer illustrated, with black crest, red jacket with light blue facings and trousers, yellow lace, wide red trouser-stripe, steel cuirass and yellow epaulettes (gold for officers). It is interesting to note that the copy of the print from which this illustration was taken shows the facings and trousers of the trumpeter's uniform to be a darker shade than those of the other ranks.

The 1st Calatrava Lancers wore helmets with black caterpillar crests; the figure illustrated is taken from a print showing probably the uniform of the élite company, distinguished by the red crest. The facings were of a crimson–red hue for the Calatrava Lancers, and of a lighter shade for the Almansa Regiment. The lance-flag illustrated was a guidon-type banner, the ordinary lance-pennons being of traditional Spanish colours, red over yellow. Trumpeters of the Calatrava Lancers wore black leather helmets of the same shape as those of the other ranks, with brass crest, front-plate, chinscales and foliage decoration on the sides, with white caterpillar crest. They wore crimson–red jackets with dark green facings (the traditional 'reversed colours' fashion), green girdle, and dark green trousers with yellow lace stripe. Trumpet-cords were mixed yellow and dark green. Note that the lancer uniform included red 'plastron'-style lapels, which do not show on the figure illustrated.

56. Britain:
a) Officer, 2nd Dragoon Guards, 1845.
b) Trooper, 1st Life Guards, 1849.

Having always been red, British heavy cavalry uniforms were unaffected by William IV's attempt to clothe the army completely in that colour. The 1831 Regulations, however, did change other details – the collars were now made entirely of the facing-colour with the red rear portion discontinued, and the single-breasted coatee was to have four lace loops on cuff and skirt for Dragoon Guards and three for Dragoons, and all officers' lace was to be gold. The closed collar adopted in 1827 was retained, but trousers changed from grey to dark blue. The 'Roman' helmet worn from 1822–23 (black leather with gilt fittings and black caterpillar crest) was changed in 1834 to an all-brass model (gilt for officers), except for the 2nd Dragoons (Royal Scots Greys) who retained their famous bearskin cap, but with the front-plate removed from about 1834.

In about 1843 another new helmet was introduced, still of all-brass but with a flowing horsehair mane. This was replaced itself in 1847 by a new pattern, the 'Albert' helmet, copied from the Prussian/Russian spiked helmet but with a horsehair plume (as worn by the 1st Life Guards trooper illustrated). Otherwise, changes in uniform were minor; in 1843 white trousers were abolished, and for a short time the 2nd Dragoons discontinued the feather plume on the fur cap; and in 1847 the coatee-skirts were shortened and squared, with officers ordered to dress in precisely the same style as the men, the coatee 'to be entirely divested of padding and stuffing'. 'Box' epaulettes remained in use for officers in full dress, with brass shoulder-scales worn by other ranks at all times and by officers in undress.

The uniform of the 2nd (Queen's) Dragoon Guards illustrated shows the 1843–47 helmet, with the regimental title borne on the label at the top edge of the peak. The 'mane', by regulation two feet ten inches long, was in some cases of a different colour for trumpeters (one contemporary picture shows white). The 'Albert' helmet, in some cases not adopted until 1850, was authorised to have black plumes for all regiments, the vari-coloured regimental patterns being first mentioned in the 1855 Regulations. The sword carried was the so-called 'scroll-hilted' pattern, with knot consisting of a white leather strap attached to a gold lace and crimson thread 'acorn'.

The 1st Life Guards trooper wears the 'Albert' helmet, which in the case of the Household Cavalry had a plate in the shape of the Star of the Order of the Garter. This figure (taken from a print by A. de Dreux) also shows the brass shoulder-scales still in use, the red flask-cord worn on the shoulder-belt, and the small cap-pouch worn on the right-hand side of the lower cuirass-strap. Shabraques at this time were much the same as used today – white sheepskin with dark blue cloth edging.

THE U.S. MEXICAN WAR, 1846–47

The expansionist policy of the United States, crystallised by the slogan 'Manifest Destiny' of the American 'right . . . to spread over this whole continent' resulted in the incorporation of the Republic of Texas into the United States, after much negotiation and at Texas' request; Mexico, controlling much of what is now south-western U.S.A., threatened war to enforce her claim to the part of Texas south of the Nueces River, the U.S. claiming that her boundary lay farther south, along the Rio Grande.

In March 1846 General Zachary Taylor with two-thirds of the regular U.S. Army (3,500 men) marched to the Rio Grande and established 'Camp Texas' opposite Matamoros and its 5,700-strong Mexican garrison. On 25 April about 1,600 Mexican cavalry crossed the river and overwhelmed a U.S. scouting party of only 63 men. Announcing that hostilities had commenced, Taylor marched to protect his supply-base at the Rio Grande mouth, and called for volunteers from Texas and Louisiana. The weakly-defended Camp Texas was immediately assaulted by General Arista's 6,000 Mexicans, but held on until Taylor returned to meet the Mexicans at Palo Alto (8 May). Arista advanced with about 4,500 men into U.S. artillery fire, and attacked with cavalry; repulsed, the Mexicans fled as Taylor's infantry advanced. Following his initial success, Taylor stormed a defence-position at Resaca de la Palma on the following day and hurled Arista's shattered force back over the Rio Grande, having lost 1,100 men to Taylor's 170.

On 13 May the United States officially declared war, and Taylor invaded Mexico on the 18th. He remained at Matamoros until August, waiting for transport and training the large number of volunteers now included in his army. Leaving 6,000 volunteers behind to complete their training, he advanced south with 3,000 regulars and 3,000 volunteers. In a hard three-day fight against 10,000 Mexicans defending Monterray, Taylor lost 488 men to the Mexican 367, but Mexican general Ampudia capitulated and marched out of the city (20–24 September). In November 1846 Taylor occupied Saltillo and was reinforced by an extra 3,000 men.

Then followed a ludicrous period of American strategical debate; General Winfield Scott planned an invasion of Mexico via Vera Cruz, but President Polk (a Democrat) was anxious that Scott (a Whig) should not become the war-hero. Polk asked Taylor to march 300 miles across the desert to San Luis Potosi and then move against Mexico City; Taylor wisely declined and supported Scott's plan. Polk reluctantly agreed, and Scott landed his army at Tampico in February 1847, some 10,000 troops including most of Taylor's regulars. The Mexican President (still Santa Anna), learning of Scott's plan by a captured message, decided to crush Taylor before Scott could move, and marched from San Luis Potosi to Saltillo, the desert-march which Taylor had declined – and wisely, as Santa Anna lost 4,000 men in a terrible winter march.

Taylor, surprised, decided to defend a narrow mountain gap at Buena Vista. On 22 February 1847 Santa Anna drove in Taylor's outposts and cut his communications by a flanking movement, then launched his main assault on the following day. Taylor's inexperienced volunteer infantry gave way, but his regular artillery performed magnificently, pouring grapeshot into the advancing Mexicans. (Here Taylor uttered his historic 'A little more grape, Captain Bragg', a heroic but probably apocryphal remark; he actually said something like 'Double-shot your guns and give 'em hell!'). The Mexicans almost reached the guns before they broke and fled; and a Mexican assault on Taylor's left was beaten off by Jefferson Davis' 1st Mississippi Volunteers. With the Mexicans recoiling in disorder, Taylor's counter-attack drove them from the field. Santa Anna withdrew completely, and the northern campaign of the war was over, ended by the brilliance of Zachary Taylor.

The U.S. 'invasion' of California (they had considerable support inside the Mexican-occupied territory) was undertaken by Commodore Stockton's naval force which occupied Monterray in June 1846; he was reinforced by a small army contingent from General Kearny's force which had captured New Mexico, and which broke through to Stockton despite a check at the Battle of Pascual (6 December 1846). Further reinforced, Kearny's combined army–navy command defeated a Mexican force at San Gabriel (9 January 1847), and California was secured for the U.S.A. Another march (like Kearny's, almost incredible by current military standards and again over 2,000 miles long) was made by Colonel Doniphan's Missouri Mounted Riflemen, marching from Santa Fé (12 December 1846) to Saltillo (21 May 1847) and defeating a large Mexican force at the Sacramento River on 28 February; Mexican losses were 600, Doniphan's only 7 killed and wounded.

In March 1847 Scott's 10,000 men landed near Vera Cruz and invested the city, which fell on 27 March after a five-day bombardment, and Scott moved inland. Santa Anna blocked his way in a seemingly-impregnable position at Cerro Gordo, but Scott discovered a mountain trail which allowed him to take the Mexicans in the flank; for the loss of 64 killed and 353 wounded, Santa Anna's much-superior force was utterly routed (18 April). When 4,000 of his volunteers went home upon the expiration of their enlistments, Scott was forced to halt until August when, reinforced, he pressed on towards Mexico City. It was an advance inviting disaster, as he was outnumbered about three to one and had deliberately abandoned his line of communications. With only four days' rations remaining, Scott attacked two heavily-defended Mexican outposts (20 August); in both battles of Contreras and Churubusco, the Mexican positions were taken, but with severe casualties; Scott lost about 1,000 (one-seventh of his force) and Santa Anna about 10,000 (including 3,000 Mexicans 'missing' – a convenient way of describing desertion!). On 8 September Scott moved closer to Mexico City, capturing the fort and gun foundry at Molino del Rey; there now only remained the fortified Chapultepec hill between Scott and Mexico City.

On 13 September the rocky heights of Chapultepec were scaled; the Mexicans resisted gallantly, including the cadets of the Military College on the hill-crest, and the San Blas coastguard battalion which died almost to a man around its colours, but the position was taken by storm and the Americans swept on to the city-gates. The assault on the Mexican capital, planned for 14 September, was unnecessary, for Santa Anna withdrew during the night and the garrison surrendered. Apart from an abortive Mexican attack on Puebla, the war was as good as over; peace was announced in February 1848, the United States gaining the territory now comprising California, Nevada, Utah, most of Arizona and New Mexico, and part of Colorado and Wyoming. President Polk's shameful political manoeuvring resulted in Scott's dismissal from command, but he was received as a national hero and awarded a gold medal by Congress – which ironically had to be presented by Polk!

The Mexican War served as a training-ground for the later Civil War (1861–65); indeed, among officers winning distinction in Mexico were Captains Robert E. Lee, Joseph E. Johnston, G. B. McClellan and Lieutenants P. G. T. Beauregard, U. S. Grant and T. J. Jackson, all of whom were to become famous during the Civil War. More than that, the Mexican War demonstrated that parade-ground uniforms had no place in active campaigning, and provided experience in the handling of full-scale campaigns involving large numbers of men, which had been lacking since the Wars of Independence and 1812.

UNIFORMS OF THE U.S.–MEXICAN WAR (Plates 57–58)

57. **Mexico:**
 a) **Private,**
 Batallon de San Blas
 (Active Coast Guards),
 1847.
 U.S.A.:
 b) **Private,**
 Infantry,
 Service Dress,
 1847.

The normal field dress of the U.S. infantry consisted of the cloth-topped forage cap (which replaced the folding leather version in 1833), with the white-braided blue-grey fatigue jacket and trousers. The cap frequently had a dark blue neck-flap which could be lowered as a protection against the sun, or could have a white 'havelock' neck-guard attached. The cap-band was officially in the arm-of-service colour (white for infantry, artillery red, dragoons yellow) which was frequently not worn, in the same way that the brass company-letter was often omitted from the front of the cap. Equipment worn on active service consisted of waist-belt with bayonet-scabbard, cross-belt and cartridge-box, black-painted knapsack, white cotton haversack, canteen and often tin cup carried on the canteen-strap.

Officers almost invariably wore dark blue frock-coats with silver-laced rank-bars and buttons, caps like those of the men but of superior quality and without the neck-curtain, light blue trousers, and carried a straight-bladed sword on a shoulder-belt. A red waist-sash was a further indication of rank. Officers usually carried only the haversack and canteen, all other equipment being carried in a shoulder-roll.

Mexican uniforms of this period were blighted by a succession of dress regulations which due to chaotic supply systems and political upheavals were frequently never implemented. The uniform shown comes from General M. A. Sanchez Lamego's 'El Batallon de San Blas 1825–55' (Mexico 1964). The San Blas Battalion of 'Active Coast Guards' originated in 1825 and led a chequered career, changing name and identity until, after serving in several rebellions and counter-coups, it was all but wiped out at Cerro Gordo, being at that time titled the 3rd Infantry Regiment. Re-organised under the old name, it stood its ground at Chapultepec hill until completely overrun; of the 400-strong battalion, only one officer and a handful of men (all wounded) managed to escape. The Colonel was found on the field of battle, wrapped in the regimental colours, shot no less than fourteen times. The uniform illustrated shows the pattern of shako normally issued to National Guard units, but as there were more than twenty authorised patterns of headdress in use in the Mexican army, it is doubtful whether the whole unit would be dressed alike. The shako bore the red, white and green national cockade and an oval plate embossed with the regimental name. The red-piped grey greatcoat was standard issue for the National Guard, only the brass collar-badge BSB identifying the unit. The red epaulettes and cuff-patches were indicative of the Grenadier company. Leather equipment was either black or white, both colours being worn indiscriminately. The firearm was still the old British 'Brown Bess' as shown in Plate 45. Officers wore dark blue frock-coats with red cuffs and collar-patches, light blue trousers with gold stripe, gold epaulettes and red waist-sash; one illustration shows an officer wearing a dark blue cloth shako, almost like a képi, with red lower band and gold lace. Other illustrations show the red collar-patch worn on the greatcoats of the other ranks in addition to the style illustrated.

58. U.S.A.:
a) Trooper, Dragoons, Service Dress, 1847.
b) Private, 1st Mississippi Rifle Volunteers, 1847.

The U.S. Dragoon uniform illustrated was that worn by regular cavalry from 1833, with the addition of the 1839 forage cap. In the Mexican War, the horse artillery and mounted riflemen wore the same uniform, with the yellow dragoon colour worn as braid and cap-band replaced by red and black-and-gold respectively. N.C.O.s wore trouser-stripes of the distinctive colour. Both in the Mexican War and on the frontier, official dragoon uniform was modified according to the fancy of the individual, the illustrated leather 'breed' leggings (named after the half-breed Indians who favoured the style) and coloured bandanas being popular; dragoons frequently cultivated shoulder-length hair and large moustaches, ear-rings were also very popular.

The 1st Mississippi Rifle Volunteers were commanded by Jefferson Davis, later to become President of the Confederate States during the Civil War. One of the best volunteer units to serve in the Mexican War, they obeyed their wounded colonel's command to 'Stand Fast' at Buena Vista, saving the American left flank from collapse; at one stage they even charged the Mexican cavalry on foot! Composed of aristocratic young southerners and accompanied by a retinue of negro slaves and servants, the regiment wore a colourful and very practical uniform – wide-brimmed straw hat, red flannel smock-shirt and white duck trousers, with regulation-pattern cartridge-boxes. Davis secured the issue of 1841 pattern percussion muskets for his regiment, thus being better-armed than even some of the regular infantry still using flintlocks. No bayonets were issued, however, each man providing his own huge knife of 'Bowie' or 'Arkansas toothpick' form, worn from a waistbelt.

THE YEAR OF REVOLUTIONS, 1848

Revolution had been fermenting in Europe for a decade or more, and in 1848 the cauldron boiled over. As one revolt occurred, it fanned the flames of others until most of the major powers were involved in one or more insurrection; some were suppressed, the revolt in France was successful, and others dragged on into full-scale wars.

A revolt in Paris in February 1848 finally toppled Louis Philippe from his precarious throne, and the Second Republic was proclaimed, itself soon tottering on the verge of collapse in the social and political unrest of the time. In the last two weeks of March, the popular uprising in Berlin known as the 'March Days' attempted to reproduce the events in France, but after some bloodshed King Frederick William agreed to concessions, and the revolt faded out.

Insurrection blazed again in Paris in June; a violent uprising of well-organised workers was put down by General Cavaignac, temporary dictator of a provisional government; ruthlessly executing the leaders of the revolt, he resigned his office, and in December Prince Louis Napoleon (nephew of Napoleon I) was elected President. In France, civil unrest was thus quelled until Louis Napoleon's coup d'état in 1851, and his appointment as Emperor in 1852.

In April 1848 Hungary, led by Lajos Kossuth, declared itself independent of Austria, and in June a Czech uprising was quelled by the bombardment of Prague by Marshal Windischgrätz's Austrian force, followed by martial control over all Bohemia. In September a Croatian army under Count Jellachich invaded Hungary to re-establish Austrian control, but was repulsed by the Hungarians who advanced over the frontier towards Vienna in October. In the previous March there had been a rising in Vienna which had forced Metternich's resignation and compelled the Emperor, Ferdinand I, to promise constitutional reforms and the relaxation of military control throughout the Empire; and now, with a Hungarian force approaching the capital, the populace of Vienna again rose in rebellion. Windischgrätz suppressed the Vienna revolt, then turned on the Hungarians and saved the capital. The Emperor, however, abdicated in favour of his nephew Franz Josef in December.

On 5 January 1849 Windischgrätz captured Budapest; the Hungarian army, having a bewildering series of changes in command, was pushed into the mountains north of Budapest, and defeated by Windischgrätz at Kápolna on 26–27 February. On 13 April the Republic of Hungary was proclaimed under President Kossuth, and the Austrians were once again driven out. Now with Russian assistance in the shape of General Paskievich's army, the Austrians under General von Haynau (who replaced Windischgrätz) invaded Hungary again in June. With the Austro–Russian armies converging, the Hungarians (commanded by General Görgei) were driven towards Transylvania. The Hungarian army in Transylvania, commanded by a Polish mercenary, General Bem, tried to take on both Austrians and Russians at once; in the Battle of Segesvar (31 July 1849) Bem's army was crushed and he retired with the remnants to join Görgei for a last stand. On 9 August Görgei was overwhelmed by Haynau's Austrians at Temesvár, withdrew in reasonable order, and surrendered to Paskievich. Haynau ended the revolt by ferocious reprisals.

Russia was also involved in the Wallachian revolt in 1848; this rebellion, related to the unrest elsewhere, was subdued by a Russian invasion. Even Scandinavia was touched by revolution; encouraged by Prussia, Schleswig-Holstein declared itself independent of Danish control, and Prussian general Wrangel marched a Prussian army into the provinces to 'protect' the state. Denmark, aided by Swedish troops, tried to re-establish control over the area and Prussia, under threat of naval action against her by Britain and with Denmark supported by both Russia and Austria, thought it prudent to retire. Deprived of Prussian support, the Schleswig-Holstein army was crushed and the revolt subdued by the Battle of Isted in 1850.

It was in Italy, however, that the bitterest fighting occurred. Following years of unrest and Austrian occupation, Milan blazed into the 'Five Days' revolt in March 1848. Bloodshed in the city ended when the 82-years old Austrian Marshal Radetzky withdrew from the city, concentrating his army of occupation in the 'fortress quadrilateral' of Mantua, Verona, Peschiera and Legnano. The Austrians went on to the defensive as an Italian coalition gathered in north Italy. On 22 March Sardinia declared war on Austria, and King Charles Albert of Sardinia assumed command of the combined Italian forces. Radetzky, with 70,000 men, fought a brilliant defensive–offensive campaign against double his strength. Encouraged by the Milan revolt, patriots in Venice under Daniele Manin declared an independent republic on 28 March 1848.

On 24–25 July 1848 Radetzky, having outmanoeuvred the Italians, crushed part of the Sardinian army at Custozza, driving the Italian forces from Lombardy, occupied Milan and besieged Venice. Garibaldi, who had served in revolutionary armies in South America following his flight when the Piedmont/Savoy uprising failed in 1834, and who had formed a volunteer army fighting in the Alps, fled to Switzerland. After a brief armistice, hostilities recommenced.

In the Papal States, Mazzini finally ousted the Pope and declared an independent Roman Republic (February 1849), but Italian forces suffered a severe setback on 23 March when Radetzky, duplicating Napoleon's tactics at Marengo, routed Charles Albert and his Polish chief of staff, General Chrzanowski at Novara; the Sardinian king abdicated in favour of his son, Victor Emmanuel II. In April, an 8,000-strong French expeditionary force under General Oudinot landed and advanced on Rome. Rome, garrisoned by 20,000 men and including 5,000 of Garibaldi's 'Legion', repulsed the first assault but was forced to capitulate. Garibaldi's contingent escaped and tried to join the besieged Venice, but pursued by French, Austrian and loyalist Italian forces, broke up and scattered; Garibaldi fled to America.

Venice had been isolated since Novara, and the condition of the besieged was desperate. After enduring great hardships from bombardment, hunger and disease, Manin surrendered (24 August). The capitulation of Venice marked the end of the War of Italian Independence (Sardinia had withdrawn from the fight on 9 August), and the conquerers of Italy exacted retribution in a savage manner, particularly the Austrian General Haynau. His cruelty – possibly magnified by Italian propaganda – led to his universal hatred throughout Europe. When his violent and continually uncontrolled temper led to his forced resignation from the Austrian army, Haynau travelled around Europe, his reputation always preceding him. He was almost killed by a mob in Brussels and when visiting London was beaten up by the draymen working in Messrs Barclay & Perkins' Brewery!

As previously described, the revolutionary movements of the 1840's produced their own 'political' uniforms, typified by the red-shirted members of Garibaldi's Legion (Plate 62). Loose clothing in the French style, smock-frocks, coloured shirts and large felt hats were all classed as 'democratic' or 'republican' uniform. That they were recognised as such is proven by numerous other nations adopting Italianate, 'republican' styles – in the United States during the Civil War, for example (including a unit known as the 'Garibaldi Guard' wearing bersaglieri uniform), and even in the 1859 volunteer movement in Britain. This political attribution even permeated official jargon: when the United States adopted the felt hat in the 1850's, it was variously styled, one of the most popular being the term 'Kossuth', named after the Hungarian patriot. As the century progressed, the combination of Franco–Prussian styles of uniform with the functionality of 'republican' costume, together with the lessons learned in the Crimean, Franco–Prussian and colonial wars, would produce a completely new theory of uniform-design. This combination of radicalism and romanticism even changed civilian costume; the days of the top-hat and tail-coat were numbered.

UNIFORMS (Plates 59–64)

59. Duchy of Modena:

a) Private,
Reali Cacciatori Scelti del Frignano (Royal Rifles of Frignano), Full Dress, 1847.

Papal States:

b) Private, Swiss Guard, Undress, 1828.

Both uniforms in this plate, though different in date and style, show the Austrian influence which spread through Italy as a result of the Austrian occupation. The Swiss Guard of the Papal States was raised in 1505 as the personal bodyguard of the Pope, a position which they still hold. Like other bodyguard corps (the British Yeomen of the Guard and the Austro-Hungarian Noble Guard for example), the Papal Guard wore an archaic uniform, scarcely changed from the Renaissance original which

legend asserts was designed by either Raphael or Michelangelo, and (as today) worn with body-armour and morion helmet in full dress. The undress version as illustrated (taken from a contemporary print) included an incongruous addition in the hat of Austrian jäger pattern. The fact that so 'modern' a head-dress should be adopted and so ruin the traditional aspect of the Swiss Guard uniform is sufficient testimony to the strength of foreign influence in uniform-design present in Italy.

The abortive 1831 revolution in Modena proved conclusively that the existing army was in no position to maintain order, so Duke Francis IV decided to put a loyalist volunteer corps raised in 1830, the 'Bersaglieri del Frignano' on to a permanent footing, and in March 1831 the unit was titled the 'Reali Cacciatori Scelti del Frignano' (Elite Royal Rifles of Frignano). The new corps, 600 strong and commanded by the Duke's son, Prince Ferdinand, was organised and equipped in the pattern of the Austrian

Tyrolean Jägers who had helped to restore order in Modena after the rebellion. After the 1848 revolution the regiment was incorporated in the Este Regiment as the 2nd (Rifle) Battalion.

The Bersaglieri del Frignano were raised in haste and there was no time to issue a uniform, only a brass badge of the F IV cypher attached to the civilian head-dress identifying its members. The 'Reali Cacciatori', however, included the typical 'round hat' with turned-up brim in their Austrian-style dress. The cock-feather plume was worn by all ranks on parade and by officers and N.C.O.s only in action; rank-marking for both commissioned and non-commissioned ranks were based on the Austrian regulations. The hat-badge, worn on the left turned-up brim, consisted of a hunting-horn with an eagle in the 'curl' of the horn, the eagle bearing a shield inscribed with the Royal cypher FV (Francis V) after Francis IV's death in 1846. This badge was also worn on the black waterproof cover which enclosed the hat in bad weather. In summer a white cloth uniform was worn on occasion, or a cotton drill version of that illustrated. Originally the corps was armed with the Austrian 'Kammer-Büchse' carbine with long bayonet, later replaced by a 'Minié' with brass-hilted sword-bayonet; later in the regiment's existence a cap-pouch was added to the intersection of the cross-belts. From the time of the Duke's exile in 1859 until their disbandment in 1863, the corps served as part of the Este Brigade in Austrian service.

60. Sardinia:
  a) 2nd Lieutenant
     with Colours,
     18th Infantry Regt
     (Acqui Brigade), 1847.
Parma:
  b) Captain,
     Guard Grenadiers,
     Full Dress, 1849–50.

This plate illustrates two 'foreign' styles used by Italian states, one Prussian and one French. Charles III of Bourbon became Duke of Parma in 1849, and immediately re-clothed his army according to the 1842–43 Prussian regulations, many uniforms and accoutrements actually being supplied by Prussia. Only in minor details did the uniforms differ from those of Prussia, principally in badges and insignia. The 'pickelhaube' is shown here in the officers' version, with horsehair plume and blue-enamelled plate; other ranks wore plain brass badges (their plates also bearing the three fleur-de-lys of Bourbon) and a spike in place of the plume, which was worn only by officers in full dress. The fleur-de-lys badge was repeated on the chinscale-boss and on the officers' epaulette-straps. Behind the chinscale-boss was worn a leather or metal painted cockade, 'quartered' in dark blue and yellow with a red border. Other ranks had similar uniforms, without the cuff-lace and with red shoulder-straps; their lace was yellow. Equipment was of Prussian pattern, of white leather, and the weapons basically French-style – the muskets used by this unit were apparently of, or similar to, the French 1842–47 percussion model.

The Sardinian officer illustrated wears a French-style uniform, with tapering shako and the blue sash common to all Sardinian units. The facings of the Sardinian infantry were arranged not by regiment but by brigade; Brigata Savoia (1st and 2nd Regiments) black, Brigate Piemonte (3rd and 4th) red, Brigata Aosta (5th and 6th) red, Brigata Cuneo (7th and 8th) crimson, Brigata la Regina (9th and 10th) white, Brigata Casale (11th and 12th) light yellow, Brigata Pinerolo (13th and 14th) black, Brigata Savona (15th and 16th) white, Brigata Acqui (17th and 18th) yellow. The flag, consisting of a white cross on a red field, was indicative of the House of Savoy, and was completed by a streamer lettered B DI ACQUIA 18 R FANTERIA (Acqui Brigade, 18th Regiment of Infantry). The colour-pole was covered in red cloth with brass studs.

61. Piedmont:
a) Officer, 16th Infantry, Campaign Dress, 1849
Milan:
b) Officer, Milan Civic Guard, 1848.

The Piedmontese infantry uniform illustrated (based on a painting of the Battle of Novara) was again in French style. Note unique additions in the scaled epaulette-straps and loosely-tied blue sash. Other details – the knee-boots and shoulder-roll worn by the officer – were additions worn on campaign. The regimental number was worn on the front of the shako.

The Milan Civic Guard uniform also contained French features (the jacket and loose trousers), but the head-dress was an Italian version of the spiked helmet, this time of steel with a black leather turban bearing a white metal cross. This white cross was a common badge on the head-dress of volunteer units during the 1848–49 war: in Venice, for example, republican volunteers wore the badge on felt hats, from which they took their name, 'Crusaders'.

A notable Italian creation of this period was the 'bersaglieri' corps (riflemen), originating from an idea of the Marquis of La Marmora of the Piedmont army, and founded in 1836. Marked from the beginning by their rapid march-pace, the bersaglieri were uniformed in the now-famous style: low-crowned, brimmed 'round hat' with cock-feather plume, dark blue tunic and trousers with crimson facings and piping, and armed with a needle-gun designed by La Marmora himself. A highly-trained, fast-moving body of marksmen, the Bersaglieri were copied by other states: in Milan, for example, National Guard Bersaglieri units wore the customary plumed hat (replaced by a képi on active service), dark green tunics with black collar, pointed cuffs and small shoulder-rolls, and grey trousers with two black stripes on the outer seams (reinforced with black leather on campaign). Armed with rifles, they carried power-flasks on green cords over the shoulder, and had black leather equipment. A brass-hilted sword-bayonet was carried on the waistbelt.

62. Roman Republic:
a) Private, Legione Italiana, 1st Uniform, 1849.
b) Lancer, Legione Italiana, 1849.
c) Private, Legione Italiana, 2nd Uniform, 1849.

The 'Legione Italiana' was the backbone of the young republic's army. Commanded by the experienced revolutionary Giuseppe Garibaldi, some of its officers were his companions from the guerrilla days in South America; the other officers and the rank and file were composed of idealists, artisans and middle-class of ardent Republican sentiment, some from other areas than Rome, adventurers – and a few convicts enlisted by Garibaldi who tried, without success to fire them with the Republican beliefs of their comrades.

When the French marched on Rome, the Triumvirate of the Republic called the Legion from its garrison-duty on the Neapolitan border to assist in the defence of the city. Some 1,300 strong, the Legion (in an attempt to capture the spirit of republican antiquity) was divided into two 'cohorts' of infantry, each comprising six 'centuries', plus cavalry and artillery companies; there was even an attempt to revive the titles 'centurion' and 'legate' for captains and lieutenants. After successfully repulsing the first French assault, Garibaldi took advantage of a truce to renew operations against Naples, but was forced to return to Rome when the French repudiated the truce. The Legion (now including a third cohort composed of Italians and foreigners) was given the most vital part of the walls to defend, the Janiculum Hill. Having lost two outposts outside the walls by a surprise night attack by the French, the Legion recovered them in the face of murderous fire – *eight times*. And eight times, the weight of numbers pushed them back. With the walls thus overlooked, the fate of Rome was sealed, but the defenders held on doggedly throughout three weeks of bombardment, assault and decimation. The final assault on the night of 29–30 June, despite a desperate counter-attack by Garibaldi's men, ended the siege. Under cover of a truce which ended the Roman Republic, Garibaldi withdrew the shattered remnants of his unit to try and carry on the fight, but to no avail.

The original uniform of the Legion, received in January 1849, consisted of a dark blue blouse with green collar, cuffs, frontal stripe and pocket-patches, worn under the greatcoat illustrated. As the supply-system varied from chaotic to non-existent, equipment usually consisted of whatever the individual soldier could find, with a black or natural leather cartridge-box worn on a leather waistbelt. As firearms were scarce at the beginning, younger members of the Legion were armed with pikes, muskets and bayonets not being universally issued until later (many of Garibaldi's 'soldiers' were 14–15 years of age). The 'Calabrian' hat was the epitome of Republican sentiments held by the Legion. In good 'democratic' fashion, all except Staff officers wore similar uniforms, company officers often being identified only by the sword with white leather knot and sometimes a red neckerchief. The staff, all Garibaldi's old comrádes, wore the red blouse of his troops in South America, plus a variety of head-dress, and used the South American saddles, knives, pistols and lassoos characteristic of that continent.

On 27 June a new uniform was adopted, consisting of a red blouse with facings as before and a panama hat, which latter item was most unpopular and soon replaced by the 'democratic' Calabrian hat. Officers adopted single-breasted red frock-coats with green collar, cuffs and piping down the front, silver buttons, light grey trousers with double green stripe, black Calabrian hat with green band, Italian tricolour cockade and black ostrich-feather; unlike those of the rank and file (which bore a hunting-horn badge), officers' waist-belt plates bore the device of a Roman eagle.

The Lancers, a group of young patriots from Bologna commanded by Angelo Masina, wore a uniform designed by themselves, consisting of black-braided blue dolman, red trousers and shako, and the skull and crossed bones badge which gave them their popular name, 'Death Lancers'. An alternative head-dress consisted of a red fez with red or blue tassel, and voluminous red trousers with black leather false boots were also worn. Swords were either straight-bladed of conventional pattern with white knot, or scimitars; horse-furniture consisted of a black sheepskin with blue

edging. The Lancers were issued with red blouses at the same time as the infantry. Many of the Lancers who had survived the eight assaults on the Janiculum Hill fell, fighting as infantry, in the final French attack.

It is interesting to note that the red shirt was originally adopted by Garibaldi's 'Italian Legion' in South America, the garments being a shipment of red tunics destined for the butchers of Buenos Aires, but diverted to clothe Garibaldi's troops!

63. Austria:
a) 'Seressaner' (Border Infantry), 1848.
b) Private, 2nd Bn, Gradisca Border Infantry Regt. (No. 8), 1848.

The Austro-Hungarian 'Grenz-Infanterie' or Border Infantry were raised in the eighteenth century, partly from Serbian and Croatian immigrants, to defend the frontiers against Turkish encroachment. Originally dressed in a semi-'native' garb, the Border infantry later adopted a style of uniform conforming to regulation pattern, but of the distinctive brown colour which contrasted sharply with the traditional Austrian white.

The figure illustrated (taken from prints by Girolamo Franceschini and others) shows the standard Austrian infantry uniform with cylindrical shako, and the tight blue breeches and 'bear's paw' cuff-lace indicative of Hungarian, rather than 'German', regiments.

Each Border regiment had a company of 'Seressaners' attached, these irregulars being employed on police duties in peace-time, and as scouts and skirmishers in war, as they were used in the 1848–49 campaigns. Their 'uniform' was virtually civilian dress, with the addition of such items as tight breeches and sometimes cloth jackets of a 'uniform' cut. Equipment was varied, being whatever the individual preferred, and weapons were equally diverse. One universal item shown in contemporary illustrations is the massive knife, two or more frequently being worn tucked behind the sash; in addition, pistols and shorter knives were much in evidence, together with either Austrian muskets or much longer, oriental-style firearms. All these weapons are shown with a profusion of brass studded decoration, bands and plates. Lace-up sandals were universal, as was the red cloth cap and the hooded cloak, a garment so common that it gave rise to the nick-name of the Seressaners, 'red-cloaks'.

Not all the Border infantry had the elegant costume shown by the figure of the 8th Regt; other contemporary prints indicate that the costume of many would have been more fitting to Transylvanian bandits than to units of the Imperial Army; an illustration of the 4th Bn the Warasdin St George Border Regt (No. 6) for example, shows an almost-Seressaner costume consisting of short brown jacket with a red waistcoat underneath, tight white breeches with brown ankle-boots, black cross-belts and a low-crowned, black 'sombrero'-type hat. Officers of the irregular units wore a costume of similar style to that of the men, but of a much finer quality and decorated with as much lace and embroidery as possible in whatever design took the wearer's fancy.

The Hungarian insurgent army of 1848–49 was based upon regular Hungarian regiments, who wore their Austrian uniforms with the sub-stitution of the new national colours of red, white and green for the black and yellow of the Austrian cockades and sashes. The Hungarian army (known as the 'Honved') wore (in general) brown skirted tunics with red frogging on the front and red piping on the collar, cuffs and around the skirts, with Austrian-style shakos and the traditional light blue breeches; artillery wore a similar uniform but with white edging and white grenade badge on the collar. Officers had gold lace and shoulder-straps of red, white and green. How-ever, a great number of irregular corps wore a motley collection of dress, with the almost-obligatory felt hat.

In the Austrian army, the tunic was introduced in 1849, with rank-badges worn upon the collar; in the field, however, the infantry generally wore plain linen jackets with collar-patches of the regimental facing colour, and had their shakos enclosed in oilskin, frequently with a white neck-curtain. The similarity in uniform between the Imperial army and that of the Honved led to a revival of the seventeenth century 'field sign' – loyal Imperial regiments signified their allegiance by a strip of white linen, worn from the chinstrap-boss, passing up to the pom-pom and down to the opposite boss, to distinguish them from the insurgent army!

64. France:
   **a) Carabinier Trumpeter,
      22nd Light Infantry,
      Service Dress, 1849.**
   **b) Voltigeur,
      22nd Light Infantry,
      Service Dress, 1849.**

This plate shows the French light infantry uniform as it was worn in Italy; the uniform worn by this regiment (and many others) was much-modified by the experiences of campaigning in Africa. The cloth képi and the greatcoat worn as, and instead of, a tunic, with the skirts often turned back to allow the legs the maximum freedom of movement, is in the style now regarded as traditional for French troops until the beginning of this century. Other innovations from African service were the method of wearing the cartridge-box at the front (it being more accessible there), and the wearing of the greatcoat turned back as lapels to show the shirt. The yellow and red epaulettes were indicative of the voltigeur and carabinier companies respectively; the blue képi with yellow piping and regimental number, and the yellow collar-patches, all indicated light infantry. This somewhat care-free appearance – in particular the fashion of turning back the lapels – met with official disapproval, to such an extent that an Order of the Day was issued on 21 June 1849 which stressed that the uniform was to be as regulation as possible. Lieutenant-Colonel Epinasse, the veteran commander of the 22nd, paid little attention; in fact some of his officers were wearing red-topped shakos instead of the cloth cap like the men.

PLATE A

(1)   (2)

179

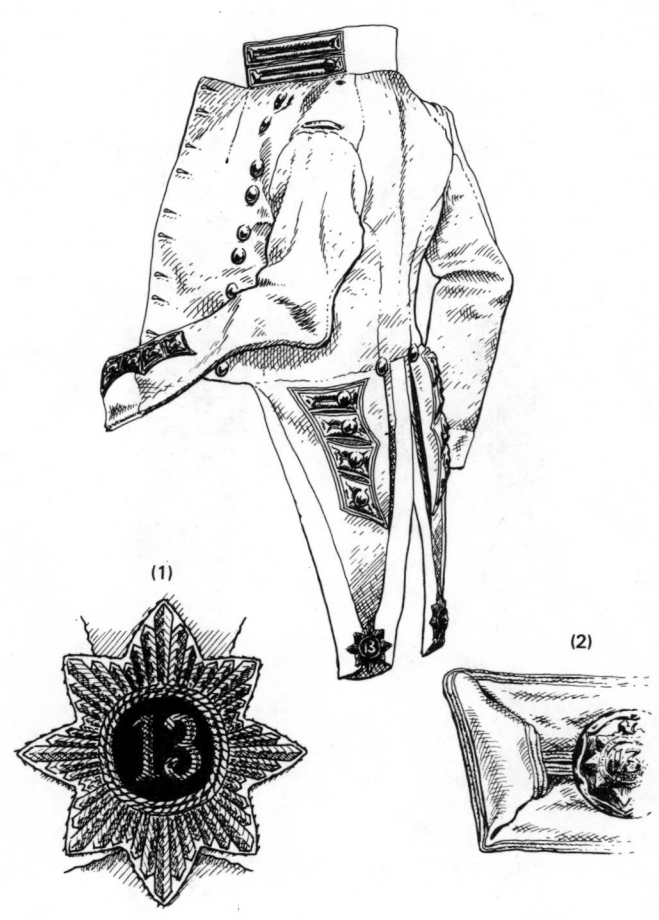

(1)

(2)

PLATE C

(2)

(1)

(3)

PLATE D

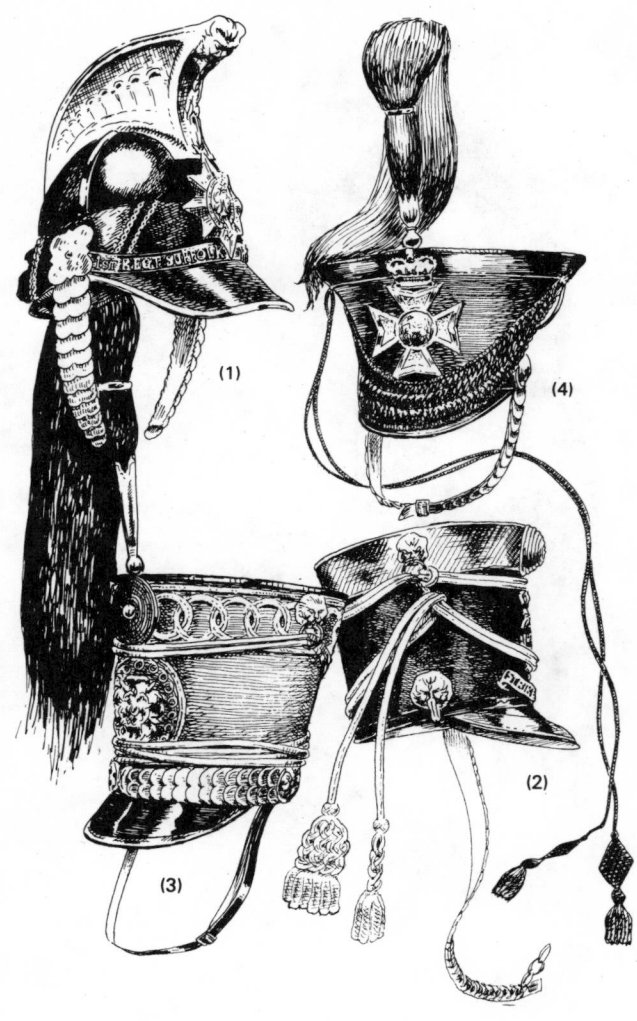

(1)

(4)

(3)

(2)

182

PLATE E

(1)

(2)

A. U.S.A. Pennsylvania Militia, 1823:
1) Private, State Guards.

Black shako with white lace lower bands and cords. White metal plate; black plume with red tip and pom-pom. Dark blue tail-less jacket with red piping around the collar, shoulder-straps, cuffs, lower edge and down breast. White lace loop on collar, white metal buttons. Black leather belts and musket-sling with white metal plates. White trousers, black boots.

2) N.C.O., Washington Blues.

Shako as before but with rectangular plate and light blue over black plume rising from white metal socket. Jacket as before, but with white piping and white, fringed shoulder-rolls. Yellow loop on collar, with red edge to loop; white chevrons. Red sash tied on right hip; white leather belts with white metal plates. Dark blue trousers, black boots; brass-hilted sabre in black leather scabbard with steel fittings. Steel halberd with light wood shaft.

(Both figures from Nesmith's 'Soldier's Manual', 1824.)

B. Indian Army. Officer's Coatee, 13th Bengal Native Infantry, 1830:

Taken from an extant item of uniform. Scarlet, with light buff facings. Gold lace and buttons (note: the upper collar-button is missing on the original). White turnbacks, with a gold-embroidered star (sketch 1) with a black cloth central portion. (2) shows design of lace. The coatee would be worn with epaulettes.

C. French Head-dress:

Taken from extant head-dress and epaulettes.
  1) Officer's helmet, Mousquetaires Noires, 1814–15.
  2) Officer's epaulette, Mousquetaires Noires, 1814–15. Worn with a silver lace 'contre-epaulette' (fringeless), of the same design.
  3) Bandmaster's shako, Infantry, c. 1825. Black beaver with black leather top, and peak, black velvet lower band. White metal fittings and white disc.

D. British Yeomanry Head-dress.
  (From extant items).
1) 1st Suffolk Yeomanry, 1828:

Black leather peak and skull, white metal fittings, black velvet turban. Plate on front in shape of Garter Star with Royal cypher in the centre. Label above peak read 1ST REGT. SUFFOLK/YEO. CAVALRY.

2) 2nd Royal Buckinghamshire Yeomanry, 1840:

Black body, silver lace, cords, and metal fittings. Front plate consisted of crowned Garter with VR cypher in the centre, with a detached scroll below in 'fretwork' letters, reading STRIKE HOME.

3) Yorkshire Hussars, 1840:

Scarlet cloth body, silver lace, cords and metal fittings. Front plate consists of a silver-plated rose in high relief, with silver lace surrounds. Black cord rosette and horsehair plume.

4) South Hertfordshire Yeomanry, 1831:

Black body with black leather upper band and peak; black cords (including festoon over peak) and plume; all fittings brass. Maltese-cross plate bears a hart in the centre.

E. Service Dress, 1846:

This plate illustrates two unusual uniforms worn on active service in North America, from contemporary pictures.

1) Shows an officer of the British King's Royal Rifle Corps, dressed for the Canadian winter in 'rifle green' with black braid, black fur cap and trimmings, and black leather equipment; 2) shows a U.S. volunteer Mounted Rifleman of the U.S.–Mexican War period, wearing buckskin shirt, trousers and moccasins, with a cloth 'poncho', coloured bandana and 'Quaker' hat.

KEY TO THUMBNAIL SKETCHES

SOURCES AND BIBLIOGRAPHY

It should be noted that a number of the illustrations may be at variance with the acknowledged details of the uniforms in question. Where this is the case, the source of the original material is given in the text. In the case of these sources being contemporary prints, the possibility exists that the original artist either misinterpreted or made errors in the details of the subject of his drawing; but equally he might have portrayed a regimentally or individually modified uniform which did not conform to authorised patterns.

Certainly, some artists are recognised as being more reliable than others; those of more dubious reputation have not been consulted for this book. For example, the many prints of Allied uniforms drawn and published in Paris during the Occupation are in general most unreliable; but even some of these contain unusual features which can be confirmed by other sources.

It should also be noted that, as it has been necessary to cover a very wide range of uniforms in this book in order the illustrate the world-wide development of military costume during the 1815–50 period, some generalisation has been necessary in the text, there being insufficient space either to enumerate the many (often conflicting) sources, or catalogue the many regimental peculiarities of corps mentioned in the text but not illustrated.

For this reason, to facilitate further reading on the subject, the bibliography has been split into two sections. As no single volume on the military costume of this period has ever before appeared, the list must necessarily include a wide range of works. Part I contains a number (though by no means a comprehensive list) of works of reference which contain a considerable amount of material on the period in question. Part II lists some of the 'secondary' sources consulted in the compilation of this book, and others which could form a basis for further research. It will be seen that a few of the sources are in the form of series of plates, and that except for notable titles, all are in English.

I

Carman, W. Y., *British Military Uniforms from Contemporary Pictures*, Hill London, 1957.

Dress Regulations 1846, Arms and Armour Press, London, 1971, facsimile reprint.

Indian Army Uniforms, Cavalry, Hill, London, 1961.

Indian Army Uniforms, Infantry, Morgan-Grampian, London, 1969.

Haswell Miller, A. E., and Dawnay, N. P., *Military Drawings and Paintings in the Royal Collection*, Vol. I (plates) and II (text), Phaidon, London, 1966 and 1970.

Haythornthwaite, P. J., *Uniforms of Waterloo*, Blandford Press, Poole, Dorset, 1974.

Kannik, P., *Military Uniforms of the World*, Blandford Press, Poole, Dorset, 1968.

Knötel, R. & H., and Sieg, H., *Handbuch der Uniformkunde*, Hamburg, 1937/1964.

Martin, P., *Der Bunte Rock (Military Costume)*, Jenkins London, and Keller, Stuttgart, 1963; Spring Books, London, 1967 (Re-issue entitled *European Military Uniforms*).

Mollo, J., *Military Fashion*, Barrie and Jenkins, London, 1972.

Nevill, R., *British Military Prints*, The Connoisseur, London, 1909.

Nicholson, Lt-Col. J. B. R., *Military Uniforms*, Orbis, London, 1973.

Thorburn, W. A., *French Army Regiments and Uniforms*, Arms and Armour Press, London, 1964.

Windrow, M., and Embleton, G., *Military Dress of North America*, Ian Allan, London, 1973.

II

Boger, A. J., *The Story of General Bacon*, Metheun, London, 1903.

Bowling, A. H., *British Hussar Regiments*, Almark, London, 1972.

Campbell, D. A., *Dress of the Royal Artillery*, Arms and Armour Press, London, 1971.

Carman, W. Y., *Head Dresses of the British Army, Cavalry*, Carman, Sutton, 1968.

Head Dresses of the British Army, Yeomanry, Carman, Sutton, 1970.

Sabretaches of the British Army, National Army Museum, London, 1969.

Demart, J., *Costumes Militaires Belges* (plates), Brussels, ...

Dupuy, R. E., and T. N., *Encyclopaedia of Military History*, Macdonald, London, 1970.

Forbes Wells, P., *De Nederlandse Cavalerie*, Van Dishoeck, Bussum, 1963.

Harvey, Lt-Col. J. R., *Records of the Norfolk Yeomanry Cavalry*, Jarrold, London, 1908.

Hayes, M. A., and Carman, W. Y., *The Costume of the 46th Regiment 1837*, National Army Museum, London, 1972.

Hefter, J., and Kannik, P., *Odd Troops Series 5 (Danish Indies)*, Mexico, 1960.

Hefter, J., *The Navy of the Republic of Texas*, Old Army Press, Colorado, 1974.

Hefter, J., *The Army of the Republic of Texas*, Old Army Press, Nebraska, 1971.

Koury, M. J., *Arms for Texas*, Old Army Press, Colorado, 1973.

Lachouque, H., *Dix Siècles de Costume Militaire*, Paris, 1963.

Lachouque, H., and Brown, A. S. K., *The Anatomy of Glory*, Lund Humphries, London, 1961.

Laffin, J., *The French Foreign Legion*, Dent, London, 1974.

Lamego, Gen. M. A. S., *El Batallon de San Blas*, Mexico City, 1964.

Linder, K., *Wojsko Polskie*, Poland.

Lord, W., *A Time to Stand*, Longmans, London, 1962.

Macrory, P., *Signal Catastrophe*, Hodder and Stoughton, London, 1966.

McBarron, H. C., *The American Soldier* (plates), Washington, 1964.

Mercer, Gen. C., *Journal of the Waterloo Campaign*, Blackwood, Edinburgh, 1870.

Miller, J., *Memoirs of General Miller in the Service of the Republic of Peru*, London, 1828.

Mollo, J. & B., *Uniforms and Equipment of the Light Brigade*, Historical Research Unit, London, 1968.

Murray, R. A., *Citadel on the Santa Fé Trail*, Old Army Press, Nebraska, 1970.

Nesmith, J. H., *The Soldier's Manual*, Philadelphia, 1824/1963.

'Q. L.', *The Yeomanry Cavalry of Worcestershire*, Devizes, 1914.

Rogers, Col. H. C. B., *Weapons of the British Soldier*, Seeley Service, London, 1960.

Shipp, J., ed., Stranks, C. J., *The Path of Glory*, Chatto and Windus, London, 1969.

Sita Ram, and Lunt, Gen. J. (trans. Norgate, J. T.), *From Sepoy to Subedar*, 1873, Routledge and Kegan Paul, 1970.

Smith, P. C., *Per Mare Per Terram*, Balfour, St. Ives, 1974.

Stadden, C. C., *The Life Guards*, Almark, London, 1973.

Thorburn, W. A., *Uniforms of the Scottish Infantry*, H.M.S.O., Edinburgh, 1970.